LIFE ON PURPOSE

A STUDY IN THE BOOK OF COLOSSIANS

www.milestonechurch.com
ISBN: 978-1-954961-19-7
Printed in the United States.

HERE'S THE PLAN

1 Grow closer to God as you understand and study His Word.

2 Study the Introduction individually. Study Weeks 1-7 with a group.

3 Discover how to live *Life on Purpose*.

HOW THIS GUIDE WORKS

Read the Chapter

CONCEPT → CONTEXT → PASSAGE → WHAT DOES THIS MEAN FOR US? → WHAT DO I DO WITH THIS?

Interact with the Concepts

TAKE NOTES IN THE MARGINS. → WRITE OUT ANSWERS TO THE QUESTIONS. → MEMORIZE THE THEME VERSE EACH WEEK.

(CARDS ARE LOCATED IN THE BACK OF THIS GUIDE.)

Talk About It with Your Group

STARTING WITH WEEK ONE:
"CHRIST *IN YOU*"

Clarification: One of God's most central character traits is His triune nature. He is One God eternally existing in three equal parts: Father, Son (Jesus), and Holy Spirit—the Trinity. Therefore, any discussion of God implies the inclusion of all three.

WHAT WE WILL COVER

Topics Like:

Purpose

Healthy Thinking

A Relationship "Masterclass"

Peace

Family

Work

& more!

Verses Like:

...so that you may live a life worthy of the Lord and please Him in every way: bearing fruit in every good work, growing in the knowledge of God. **Colossians 1:10**

To them God has chosen to make known among the Gentiles the glorious riches of this mystery, which is Christ in you, the hope of glory. **Colossians 1:27**

So then, just as you received Christ Jesus as Lord, continue to live your lives in him. **Colossians 2:6**

For you died, and your life is now hidden with Christ in God. **Colossians 3:3**

Whatever you do, work at it with all your heart, as working for the Lord, not for human masters. **Colossians 3:23**

COLOSSIANS READING PLAN

This guide does not go through Colossians verse by verse,
but instead covers the major themes as we make our way through the entire letter.

WE ENCOURAGE YOU TO CHOOSE 1 OF THE 2 FOLLOWING READING PLANS.

FOLLOW THE SERIES:
(MORE READING WITH REPETITION)

INTRO Week: Colossians 1

Week 1: Colossians 1 & 2

Week 2: Colossians 3

Week 3: Colossians 3

Week 4: Colossians 3

Week 5: Colossians 3

Week 6: Colossians 3

Week 7: Colossians 4

FINISH BY THE END:
(LESS READING)

Week 1: Colossians 1:1–14

Week 2: Colossians 1:15–23

Week 3: Colossians 1:24–2:5

Week 4: Colossians 2:6–23

Week 5: Colossians 3:1–17

Week 6: Colossians 3:18–4:1

Week 7: Colossians 4:2–18

CONTENTS

INTRODUCTION **9**

Week 1: CHRIST *IN YOU* **31**

Week 2: YOUR *THINKING* **53**

Week 3: YOUR *RELATIONSHIPS* **73**

Week 4: YOUR *PEACE* **93**

Week 5: YOUR *FAMILY* **113**

Week 6: YOUR *WORK* **135**

Week 7: MAKE THE *MOST* OF *EVERY* OPPORTUNITY **157**

Intro Week

INTRODUCTION

THEME VERSE

To them God has chosen to make known among the Gentiles the glorious riches of this mystery, which is Christ in you, the hope of glory.

Colossians 1:27

KEY TRUTH

Life on Purpose is intentional, meaningful, and comes from the One who created us.

PASSAGE

Colossians 1:27

CONCEPT

MAYBE IT STARTS WITH *a small suspicion.*

MAYBE IT'S *a hunch you can't shake.*

MAYBE IT'S *hard for you to describe*, BUT *deep down you know it's true.*

For many of us, this sense goes back as far as we can remember.

A profound conviction . . . there has to be more to life.

A better life.

"The Good Life."

The life we were created to live.

So, the question becomes: How do you find this life?

And for that matter: Where does it come from?

Every person wrestles with these questions because they're a big part of being human.

That's why we've called this study ***Life on Purpose***.

We know this life we're looking for requires intentionality. We can't stumble into it. We won't find it by looking to ourselves.

Most of us tend to evaluate how we're doing during big transitions and new seasons:

- **We start our first year at college.**
- **We move to take a new job.**
- **We get married.**
- **We start a business.**
- **We bring our first (or second, third, or fourth!) child home from the hospital.**

All of these moments can be the exciting fulfillment of prayerful decisions. Once they've happened and have become our daily routine, we often wonder, *Am I living the best version of my life?*

Am I living *Life on Purpose*?

In this study on the book of Colossians, we will learn where this purpose comes from, how to find it, and how it changes our thinking, our relationships, our families, and even our workplace.

✦✦✦

Right now, at this moment, our lives are happening. And because life is unfolding in real time, it's messy. It's rarely linear or uniform.

Life is not a movie that follows a tightly-crafted script that has been carefully edited, brilliantly directed, and scored with a moving soundtrack for maximum emotional impact.

And so, we're left to try and make sense of the mystery of our existence.

We all live in this tension:

- **The life I want versus the life I'm actually living.**
- **A life of significance versus a life where nothing seems to matter.**
- **A *Life on Purpose* versus a life that happens to me.**

Culture and conventional wisdom have responded to this challenge by suggesting we can write our own stories:

"We can live our truth."
"We can 'manifest' what we want."
"We're the masters of our fate—the captains of our destiny."

?

Am I living *Life on Purpose?*

It sounds so promising.

Have you ever noticed those people on Instagram or TikTok who look like they have perfect lives? They go on the best vacations, stay at the nicest places, and eat the best meals.

Everything in their lives is carefully curated to look amazing. Which makes us wonder, *Is this real?* If you look closely, you can almost catch them wondering too.

Our appetite for this kind of life far exceeds what people are actually experiencing.

We have more options, more information, more opportunities, and yet, we are more anxious than ever.

Personal technology allows us to live in a perpetual state of connection, yet loneliness (especially among young people) is at an all-time high.

Perhaps the only thing more difficult than really wanting something is getting it and realizing it can't deliver what it promised. You set an ambitious goal, you work really hard to achieve that goal, and then once you have it, you discover you don't feel much different.

This common experience is known as "the arrival fallacy."

It turns out we may not be the best judges. Our expectations have a significant impact on our outcomes. Even when we get everything our hearts desire, we often turn up empty.

There is a direct correlation between prioritizing and fixating on our personal happiness and perpetually feeling unhappy.

The fastest way to become unhappy is to reduce your life to the pursuit of happiness.

But we keep trying anyway.

We seem to think we're one "aha moment" away from discovering everything we've always wanted.

Self-help is a multibillion-dollar industry that remains wholly incapable of fulfilling its promises.

In other words (despite the non-stop insistence of culture), looking inside to find ***Life on Purpose***—happiness, fulfillment, and significance—very well may be the worst place to look.

✦ ✦ ✦

The book of Colossians is a letter written by the apostle Paul to a group of Christians in the town of Colossae. Paul had never been there, but he had heard all about this great church from his friend Epaphras who started it.

The Holy Spirit supernaturally inspired Paul with the right words to encourage followers of Christ—both the actual people

THE FASTEST WAY TO BECOME UNHAPPY IS TO REDUCE YOUR LIFE TO THE PURSUIT OF HAPPINESS.

who first received the letter, as well as any of us who read it later.

In this letter, Paul describes the life we're looking for as "the hope of glory."

This may be hard for us to understand, but it contains everything we're looking for.

We understand the *hope* part. Hope is a powerful force; it inspires us to keep going, to never quit, to fix our eyes on something we do not have but believe we can receive.

Hope makes us vulnerable because hope creates expectations that can lead to disappointment. But hope also strengthens and emboldens us because it reminds us the story is not over.

We may not always have hope, but we understand what it is.

Glory is a word that can be more difficult for us to understand.

When the Bible uses the word "glory," it's much bigger than fame or fortune. Glory is more than a standing ovation or the celebration given to a victor.

To them God has chosen to make known among the Gentiles the glorious riches of this mystery, which is Christ in you, the hope of glory.

Colossians 1:27

Glory comes from God. Glory rightfully belongs to God.

In Hebrew, the word "glory" is literally translated as "weight." There is a depth and substance to glory that's bigger than celebratory confetti or fireworks.

Anything with great weight is not easily moved or changed.

When we think about the meaning, the depth, the fulfillment, and the substance of the good life—the life we were created to live—what we're struggling to describe is glory.

And Paul says that there's only one way to find this hope of glory: Jesus comes and lives on the inside of us.

This is *Life on Purpose*: when Jesus comes and lives in us, He changes the areas of our lives we care about the most.

Colossians 1:10 says this way of living is worthy of the Lord and pleases Him in every way as we bear fruit in every good work and grow in our understanding of God.

To bear fruit is to produce good things in our lives and to add value to the lives of others. We're no longer drifting through life. Our lives have purpose and meaning.

We find significance in the day-to-day, ordinary moments because we're doing them out of our love for Jesus.

So that you may live a life worthy of the Lord and please him in every way: bearing fruit in every good work, growing in the knowledge of God.

Colossians 1:10

✦ ✦ ✦

Saul (who was later referred to by his Greek name, Paul, starting in Acts 13:9) was driven and accomplished. He came from a respected Jewish family, studied under the best rabbis (teachers), kept all the requirements of the Jewish law, and ruthlessly opposed and persecuted the earliest followers of Christ.

But then Saul met the resurrected Jesus on the road to Damascus and everything changed.

He gives up his whole life to follow Jesus.

He finds his purpose and meaning in pursuing this calling from heaven. Despite persecution, imprisonment, beatings, and the constant threat of death, Paul says everything else is worth nothing compared to knowing and loving Jesus.

[3] As he neared Damascus
on his journey, suddenly a
light from heaven flashed
around him. [4] He fell to the
ground and heard a voice say
to him, "Saul, Saul, why do
you persecute me?" [5] "Who
are you, Lord?" Saul asked.
"I am Jesus, whom you are
persecuting," he replied. [6]
"Now get up and go into the
city, and you will be told what
you must do."

Acts 9:3-6

CONTEXT

When Paul writes his letter to the church in Colossae, he is in prison and this church is in danger of false teaching and destructive lies.

And yet the letter serves as a beacon of hope and encouragement.

Scholars believe Epaphras heard Paul's preaching in Ephesus and became a faithful disciple before returning to Colossae and telling his friends and family about this Jesus Paul spoke about. It took the average traveler about a week on foot to go from the large coastal city of Ephesus to the remote inland town of Colossae (both were located in what we know as the modern nation of Turkey).

LOCATIONS OF SEVERAL NEW TESTAMENT CHURCHES

PAUL WRITES LETTERS TO CHURCHES IN:

Colossae (Colossians)

Ephesus (Ephesians)

Philippi (Philippians)

Thessalonica (1 & 2 Thessalonians)

Corinth (1 & 2 Corinthians)

Rome (Romans)
not pictured

Paul rejoices with this body of believers because of their faith in Jesus and their love for all of God's people. More than adopting a religious philosophy, the Colossians embraced the gospel with their whole lives.

Epaphras was an exceptional leader. His name means "charming," and he's described as beloved, a servant, and a faithful minister. Paul knew Epaphras modeled this approach for these new believers. He did far more than give them spiritual information—he loved, served, and prayed for them with all the strength he had.

Paul calls Epaphras his fellow worker, fellow soldier, and fellow prisoner. Instead of being anxious or afraid, these imprisoned men who were facing death provided tremendous encouragement and hope for the people in this church who found themselves without their primary leader.

The word was out on what was happening in this remote inland town, and people were coming to check it out. Not only had the Colossians attracted Paul's attention, but there were also false teachers and opponents of the gospel who viewed what was happening as an opportunity for their own selfish agenda.

Like many of the other churches in the New Testament, one of the first dangerous lies they encountered was the idea that faith in Jesus was not enough.

In fact, when you study the earliest followers of Jesus, all of

> 7 You learned it from Epaphras, our dear fellow servant, who is a faithful minister of Christ on our behalf, 8 and who also told us of your love in the Spirit.
>
> **Colossians 1:7-8**

the wrong views and misunderstandings always come back to the failure to see Jesus for who He really is.

These problems are still with us today. Here are a few of the more common ones:

- "Jesus was a good teacher with solid spiritual principles."
- "Jesus is one of many paths to God."
- "If Jesus helps you, that's fine. But you can't say He is better than any other religious tradition or belief system."

This tone sounds so caring and mature, but it completely contradicts the entirety of Paul's life. Accordingly, the first part of Paul's letter is radical, intense, and doesn't align with this way of thinking.

Paul separates Jesus from every other person in human history and describes Him with words and phrases that are incompatible with the ideas listed above.

The BIG idea of Colossians is the supremacy of Christ—this is a formal way of saying Jesus is better and different than anyone else who has ever lived.

He was more than a spiritual leader or a religious teacher. He was fully God . . . and He came and lived among us as one of us. And then He died and rose again so we could be restored to a perfect relationship with God for all eternity.

This, and only this, is the way to a ***Life on Purpose.***

He is the image of the invisible God. To see Jesus is to see God. He is the firstborn over all creation—everything belongs to Him.

And just in case it's not entirely clear: ***All things have been created THROUGH Him and FOR Him.***

15 The Son is the image of the invisible God, the firstborn over all creation. 16 For in him all things were created: things in heaven and on earth, visible and invisible, whether thrones or powers or rulers or authorities; all things have been created through him and for him.

Colossians 1:15-16

THE BIG IDEA *of Colossians* IS THE *SUPREMACY OF CHRIST*—THIS IS A FORMAL WAY OF SAYING *Jesus is better* AND *different* THAN *anyone else* WHO HAS *ever lived.*

Colossians 1:27

[NIV] To them God has chosen to make known among the Gentiles the glorious riches of this mystery, which is Christ in you, the hope of glory.

[CEB] God wanted to make the glorious riches of this secret plan known among the Gentiles, which is Christ living in you, the hope of glory.

[MSG] This mystery has been kept in the dark for a long time, but now it's out in the open. God wanted everyone, not just Jews, to know this rich and glorious secret inside and out, regardless of their background, regardless of their religious standing. The mystery in a nutshell is just this: Christ is in you, so therefore you can look forward to sharing in God's glory. It's that simple.

[NLT] For God wanted them to know that the riches and glory of Christ are for you Gentiles, too. And this is the secret: Christ lives in you. This gives you assurance of sharing his glory.

WHAT DOES THIS MEAN FOR US?

Only God can use a letter from a guy in prison to a church he never visited and connect it to us today.

Human nature and our deepest longings have not changed. We're all still looking for the good life. We all want purpose and meaning.

Many of us who are driven and accomplished are all too familiar with the reality of the arrival fallacy. We got the prize, but we don't feel fulfilled.

We're looking for glory in the wrong ways and places.

That's why Paul calls it a "mystery." Most Jewish people were waiting for the Messiah who would come and redeem Israel. Most of them missed that Jesus was this long-awaited Savior.

The other mystery is that this Jewish Messiah would not just come to redeem and restore Israel, but all people everywhere.

The glorious riches of Christ coming and living inside of you are now available to anyone, anywhere, who would simply receive Him.

Nothing in life is more important.

One other thing about this church in Colossae stands out. Within a few short years of Paul's letter, there was a massive earthquake in Colossae. We don't know exactly what happened, but the town fades from historical reference.

Later in the New Testament when churches are listed, this wonderful group of believers is not included.

To our modern sensibilities, this appears tragic.

However, when you think about it, what an incredible picture of God's goodness and grace!

After all, while the town of Colossae may have disappeared thousands of years ago, its legacy continues to encourage and strengthen people all over the world to this day.

What God did in their lives, and their loving and faithful response to it, continues to have meaning, depth, and purpose even now.

This life is a breath. Cities rise and fall. We get one shot at this life, and it's a flame that burns quickly.

What Do I Do with This?

You have to start with a growth mindset—I want to learn, I want to grow, and I'm open to what God wants to do.

- **It doesn't matter if we grew up going to church.**
- **It doesn't matter what our religious background was . . . or wasn't.**
- **It doesn't matter if we've made mistakes and done things we're not proud of because none of us can earn or demand a right relationship with God.**

What matters is the posture of our hearts toward Jesus, who is unlike anyone else in human history.

God wants you to grow and become everything He created you to be.

The true you—the best version of who you were created to be—is hidden in Christ.

For you died, and your life is now hidden with Christ in God.

Colossians 3:3

In order to find it, you don't go deeper into yourself—you go deeper into Him. This is counterintuitive and against every impulse of the world.

Your feelings and experiences can easily become an obstacle.

If we want to share in the encouragement, faith, and joy of the Colossians, we have to be willing to do what they did.

We cannot view a relationship with Jesus as helpful spiritual information. We have to allow it to impact every area of our lives.

It's not enough to know about Jesus. We have to know Him ourselves.

Prayer

Lord, I know ***Life on Purpose*** is intentional, meaningful, and comes from You. As I begin this journey, help me to hear You clearly so I can discover the life You have for me. In Jesus' name, Amen.

Week One

01.

CHRIST *IN YOU*

THEME VERSE

He is the one we proclaim, admonishing and teaching everyone with all wisdom, so that we may present everyone fully mature in Christ.

Colossians 1:28

KEY TRUTH

Life on Purpose is only found in Christ.

PASSAGE

Colossians 2:6-10, 13

CONCEPT

WE ALL WANT TO KNOW ***our purpose.*** ALL OF US HAVE WONDERED, ***What am I here for?***

IT'S A QUESTION WE ***revisit throughout our lives*** BECAUSE WE BELIEVE ***there is an answer.***

Fulfillment and significance are always attached to meaning.

And if you want to know the meaning of something, you have to ask the one who designed it.

Do you remember the first time you heard the term *Wi-Fi*? What about a *smartphone*? What about the *internet*?

Those who are younger will never fully comprehend a time when these things didn't dominate our daily lives.

Those of us old enough to remember life without them relate to them differently.

Believe it or not, there was a time when human beings had the same feelings about the television, the radio, and even books.

Whenever we are introduced to something new, our excitement and willingness to learn are dependent upon our understanding of the object's purpose.

Human beings are not objects, but we also experience a much greater level of joy and well-being when our lives have clear significance and meaning.

We don't do well without them. In much the same way, Paul says: ***The only way for us to discover our purpose is to ask the One who created us.***

Paul goes to great lengths to describe the uniqueness and supremacy of Christ. There's no one like Him. He's not one option among many. He stands alone.

He is the one we proclaim, admonishing and teaching everyone with all wisdom, so that we may present everyone fully mature in Christ.

Colossians 1:28

That's why Paul continually brings the reader back to Jesus. He is the whole point. He is the One we proclaim.

Paul says, "I'll teach you, admonish you, encourage you, give you all the wisdom I've got for one simple purpose: to present you fully mature in Christ."

Paul had never met these people. He's in prison, so he's not sure if he ever will. This may be his only communication with them.

So he does everything he can to show them what's most important—you've got to know who Jesus is.

Jesus alone offers us *Life on Purpose.*

Jesus alone offers us *Life on Purpose.*

Despite what the best minds in marketing may tell us, we weren't created to live with the total absence of difficulty or discomfort.

It can be easy to assume our purpose, the life we've always wanted, is waiting for us to stumble upon it like the perfect person we're destined to be with. If we keep looking, eventually we'll find them.

But what if challenges and adversity are not signs that life is broken or we're wasting our time doing the wrong things? What if they're necessary ingredients to our growth and development?

> 2 Dear brothers and sisters, when troubles of any kind come your way, consider it an opportunity for great joy. 3 For you know that when your faith is tested, your endurance has a chance to grow. 4 So let it grow, for when your endurance is fully developed, you will be perfect and complete, needing nothing.
>
> **James 1:2-4 (NLT)**

Outside of a much-needed day off or the occasional vacation, doing nothing does not satisfy us at a deep level. And let's be honest, when was the last time you described your vacation as doing nothing? We try to cram so many things into these moments and often come back more tired than when we left.

Our culture confuses busyness or activity with purpose. It's far too easy to fall into the routine of viewing being "busy" as being significant or fulfilled.

They are not the same.

We live in the most individualistic era in human history. More than our commitments, our responsibilities, our families, or our faith, we value personal freedom and expression.

Culture shouts from the rooftops: "Follow your heart! Live your truth. Chase your dreams. You do YOU!"

There is this prevailing notion that if we slowed down and looked inward, each of us would be able to find our true selves. If only we weren't so busy, then we would be able to discover our purpose.

It sounds so noble. The problem is, it doesn't work.

It does not produce what we're looking for.

Much like the pursuit of happiness, being hyper-driven and fixating on our purpose doesn't lead to the desired outcomes.

Remember, Paul was driven. He knew what it was like to achieve goals. And yet, he continually steers us deeper into Christ, not into our own interests and feelings.

✦✦✦

Perhaps the idea that "Christ in us" is the thing we're all really looking for sounds like a religious platitude—like something religious people say because they don't have an answer and they're scared to look.

Maybe it sounds corny.

Historical context helps us here. Paul lost everything for Jesus—his position, his influence, his connections, and his mentors and teachers.

He is not writing from a spiritual retreat center—he's writing from jail.

He spent the majority of his ministry suffering, often beaten and attacked by the people he was serving, and in constant trouble with the governing authorities.

Not because his ideas were easily dismissed and inconsequential. But precisely because his preaching was disruptive everywhere he went. These were more than untested theories or vague concepts to Paul.

He was a world expert in the minutiae of the hundreds of laws concerning Jewish religious worship practices. These were observed on a daily basis with painstaking detail out of reverence for God—especially since messing some of them up occasionally led to death on the part of the worshiper.[1]

I, Paul, write this greeting in my own hand. Remember my chains. Grace be with you.

Colossians 4:18

[1] Check out the wild stories of Uzzah (2 Samuel 6:1-7) and Ananias & Sapphira (Acts 5:1-11)!

For example, God's presence was so holy, so pure, and so "other" that He would only come near the people one day per year. There were extravagant requirements only the high priest could fulfill so he could spend a brief moment in the Holy of Holies where God's presence came down.

Paul understood this as well as anyone on the planet. So, when he writes that the mystery that was hidden for ages and generations is now being made known to all the Lord's people, it's a really big deal.

The glorious mystery is that this Holy God, who could only be worshiped under the strictest requirements, by the chosen high priest of Israel, on the holiest day of the year... was now making His home and living on the inside of any person who would receive Jesus and put their trust in Him.

When this God comes and lives on the inside of us, He changes us. He gives us purpose and meaning. He calls us to live a life worthy of Him—one that pleases Him in every way.

The way this happens is less about *the what* and more about *the how.*

As we study Paul's letter to this amazing church, we'll realize that discovering our purpose is less like discovering a mission in a secret file and more like following a trail of breadcrumbs until we look up one day and realize the incredible things God has done in us and through us.

But only the high priest entered the inner room, and that only once a year, and never without blood, which he offered for himself and for the sins the people had committed in ignorance.

Hebrews 9:7

CONTEXT

The tone of Paul's letter picks up its urgency in the second chapter. He explains that his goal for them is to know the mystery of God made known in Jesus, in whom are hidden all of the treasures of wisdom and knowledge.

Paul is concerned for the well-being of these new believers because he doesn't want them to be deceived by "fine-sounding" arguments.

Later, he explains these arguments come from empty and hollow philosophies based on human tradition and spiritual forces.

While scholars debate the specifics of these philosophies and whether they came from traditional Jewish groups or a sect of Jewish spiritualists, the primary lie they were spreading was that faith in Jesus was not enough to make you right with God. They insisted true devotion required adherence to dietary laws, observation of the Sabbath, and New Moon festivals.

Jews snuck into the church and told these new Christians they had to adhere to the strict rules—what they did or didn't eat and drink, how they observed the Sabbath, and which religious festivals they did or didn't participate in.

These may sound irrelevant or insignificant to us, but trust and faith don't come easily to human beings. We like external spiritual activities we can point to that make us feel holy or special. For instance:

- I go to church every week.
- I read my Bible every day.
- I regularly serve people in need.

These may be wise choices that improve the quality of our lives, but none of them make us right with God, or spiritually superior to our neighbor.

And while these may sound spiritual, they are not the message of Jesus.

As Colossians 2:13-15 says, when we were dead in our sin and transgressions, God made us alive in Christ, forgiving our sins and canceling the charges against us.

In Colossians 2:6-7, Paul reminds them of the simple beauty

13 When you were dead in your sins and in the uncircumcision of your flesh, God made you alive with Christ. He forgave us all our sins, 14 having canceled the charge of our legal indebtedness, which stood against us and condemned us; he has taken it away, nailing it to the cross. 15 And having disarmed the powers and authorities, he made a public spectacle of them, triumphing over them by the cross.

Colossians 2:13-15

and purity of the gospel: "So then, just as you received Christ Jesus as Lord, continue to live your lives in him, rooted and built up in him, strengthened in the faith as you were taught, overflowing with thankfulness."

To be a follower of Christ and to have Christ in you means you believe He knows you better than you know yourself.

It is the conscious choice to put your trust in His righteousness instead of your own.

And it is the decision to look to Jesus to discover your purpose instead of choosing your own purpose and then asking God to bless what you've decided.

Colossians 2:6-10, 13

6 So then, just as you received Christ Jesus
as Lord, continue to live your lives in him,
7 rooted and built up in him, strengthened in the
faith as you were taught, and overflowing with
thankfulness.

8 See to it that no one takes you captive through
hollow and deceptive philosophy, which depends on
human tradition and the elemental spiritual forces
of this world rather than on Christ.

9 For in Christ all the fullness of the Deity lives in
bodily form, 10 and in Christ you have been brought
to fullness. He is the head over every power and
authority. . . .

13 When you were dead in your sins and in the
uncircumcision of your flesh, God made you alive
with Christ. He forgave us all our sins.

WHAT DOES THIS MEAN FOR US?

It's not religion. It's not self-help. It's not about spiritual effort or willpower. It's not about impressing others through external obedience.

We enter our relationship with Jesus by grace through faith. It's a gift we cannot earn. It's not something we strive for or find by sheer willpower.

We have nothing to offer Him, yet He gives everything to us.

We don't negotiate. We surrender.

We freely admit He knows us better than we know ourselves. And so, our response is to live our whole lives in Him.

Our hope of glory, our purpose, is to allow His presence to transform our lives beyond our weekly worship service.

[8] For it is by grace you have been saved, through faith—and this is not from yourselves, it is the gift of God— [9] not by works, so that no one can boast.

Ephesians 2:8-9

To be "in Christ" means to experience His empowering presence in every area of our lives. This is not something reserved for pastors or a select few professional Christians. It is available for all of God's people.

Paul compares this way of life to being "rooted in Christ,"— all growth comes from our relationship with Him.[2]

And then he identifies two key ingredients to this way of life: 1) strong faith and 2) overflowing thankfulness.

Faith is the conviction of what we can't see. It's unwavering trust. A confidence in the character and goodness of God.

Thankfulness is a general posture where we remember that everything we have is a gift from this good and loving God who is always working on our behalf.

When we put all of our faith and trust in what Jesus did for us, we receive the full benefits of the power of the cross.

These include disarming and triumphing over all of the spiritual forces of darkness.

This causes us to overflow with gratitude and thanksgiving, because of everything Jesus has made possible through His death and resurrection.

Now faith is the assurance of things hoped for, the conviction of things not seen.

Hebrews 11:1 (ESV)

[2] Paul is referencing one of the most famous psalms here, Psalm 1:3, where the person who meditates on God's Word every day is compared to a tree planted by the water, who bears fruit in season, and whose leaves never wither.

WHEN WE PUT *all of our faith* AND *trust in* WHAT *Jesus did* FOR US, WE RECEIVE *the full* BENEFITS OF THE *power* OF *the* CROSS.

What Do I Do with This?

Whatever we're rooted in will fill our lives.

Whatever we're "in" at the deepest level is what comes out of us.

To be "in Christ" means our foundations are rooted in who He is and what He values. And because our deepest connections are in Him, what comes out of our lives looks like Him.

If we're "in our career," we may occasionally feel joy and fulfillment when things are good, but we'll also be subject to a lot of frustration and disappointment.

If we're "in our spiritual performance," we'll wear ourselves out trying to prove our worth to God (and ourselves), and we'll be trapped constantly comparing ourselves to everyone else.

In John 15, Jesus told His disciples that He was the vine and they were the branches. He told them that apart from Him, they could do nothing. But if they remained (or abided) in Him, they would bear fruit that would always remain.

That same promise is available to us.

To be in Christ is more than a religious formality. It's more than a box you check.

To be in Christ is to make the conscious decision to begin each day inviting His presence to impact every area of our lives.

Through this study we will practically learn how to be in Christ:

- **In the way we think and speak.**
- **In all of our relationships.**
- **In our pursuit of peace.**
- **In the way we love and serve our family.**
- **In the way we act in the workplace.**
- **In the way we treat people who are different from us.**

This is what it means to live *Life on Purpose*.

---

5 "I am the vine; you
are the branches. If you
remain in me and I in
you, you will bear much
fruit; apart from me
you can do nothing...
7 If you remain in me
and my words remain
in you, ask whatever
you wish, and it will be
done for you. 8 This is to
my Father's glory, that
you bear much fruit,
showing yourselves to
be my disciples."

John 15:5, 7-8

Discussion

Read Colossians 2:6-7: [6] So then, just as you received Christ Jesus as Lord, continue to live your lives in him, [7] rooted and built up in him, strengthened in the faith as you were taught, and overflowing with thankfulness.

1. What do you think it means to be "in Christ"?

2. What does it mean to be "rooted in Christ"? What does the image of being "rooted" make you think of?

3. What are some of the wrong areas in which we try to root ourselves? Why are these dangerous?

4. How can we be "built up" in Christ?

5. Why are faith and thankfulness key ingredients to life in Christ?

6. Which area do you need to grow in more: faith or thankfulness? Explain.

7. Where does purpose in life ultimately come from?

Questions

Application

How would you describe your relationship with God right now?

Are you in Christ, rooted and established?

What can you do to become more rooted in Christ?

Prayer

Jesus, I believe ***Life on Purpose*** is only found in You. I want to know You more. Please give me eyes to see You and ears to hear You. In Your name I pray, Amen.

Week Two

02.

YOUR *THINKING*

THEME VERSE

For you died, and your life is now hidden with Christ in God.

Colossians 3:3

KEY TRUTH

Life on Purpose requires us to align our thoughts with God's Word.

PASSAGE

Colossians 3:1-10

CONCEPT

HERE'S A THOUGHT EXPERIMENT FOR YOU: ***Don't think about*** TINY, PINK, DANCING ***elephants.***

YOU'RE THINKING ***about them, aren't you?***

Isn't it interesting how the mere mention of something creates a thought in our minds? Our thoughts fill our minds. Our minds influence our hearts. And our hearts always impact our actions.

In other words:

Whatever we focus on fills our lives.

We live in an unprecedented moment in human history. We have access to more information in a single day than previous

Life on Purpose requires us to align our thoughts with God's Word.

generations encountered in a year or a decade.

For many of us, managing this information leads to stress, anxiety, and worry.

We don't have to seek these things out—they come looking for us through push notifications, robocalls, blanket text messages, and spam emails.

Without an intentional plan, these seemingly insignificant patterns can end up having a major impact on the quality of our lives.

Before we realize it, our mental health is deteriorating simply because life is happening to us. We have to consider which voices we're going to listen to.

We have to decide who we're going to trust because the voices we listen to end up shaping the direction of our lives.

Almost 2,500 years ago, the Greek philosopher Socrates summarized it this way: "The unexamined life is not worth living."

All of us need to spend a little more time thinking about what we're thinking about.

✦ ✦ ✦

Life on Purpose requires us to align our thoughts with God's Word.

This is a process that happens over time, but we commit to it every day. We begin by inviting Jesus into our thoughts to challenge our thinking and influence our mindsets.

We all have a little voice in our heads. It sounds like us. We think it's us. But that little voice is constantly receiving input from all kinds of places, and that input produces a wide variety of thoughts.

If we listen to and act on every thought that pops into our minds, we're in trouble. When we commit our lives to Jesus, we give Him first right of refusal in our thoughts because we believe the life we're looking for is found in Him, not in us.

Paul takes it a step further. He doesn't say to try your best to put Jesus first. Instead, he says that when we give our lives to Christ, the old version of us dies.

The new version, the one we've been looking for, is hidden in Christ.

For you died, and your life is now hidden with Christ in God.

Colossians 3:3

We don't save ourselves or make ourselves new. Jesus does that part. But we're the only ones who can make the choice to say no when those old thoughts and habits try to creep back in.

This requires our active engagement, not our passive agreement.

We have to take our thoughts captive. We have to evaluate the source of the ideas that impact us on a regular basis.

We demolish arguments and every pretension that sets itself up against the knowledge of God, and we take captive every thought to make it obedient to Christ.

2 Corinthians 10:5

We need to examine them in light of God's Word (the Bible) to see if they can be trusted. Of course, this requires us to know what God's Word says.

The new believers in Colossae didn't have Wi-Fi, smartphones, social media, or internet access. And yet, they had plenty of things to worry about.

Paul challenges them to stop thinking so much about the opinions of their peers, the philosophies of religious experts, and the constant drama and chatter of their culture.

Instead, because they have been raised with Christ, because all the treasures of wisdom and knowledge are hidden in Him, they must set their minds on things above, not on earthly things.

This is not our natural tendency. Human beings tend to take on the beliefs and attitudes of the people they spend the most time with.

And earthly things come from our earthly nature, which quickly becomes tempted by evil desires that promise a thrilling version of the good life.

[1] Since, then, you have been raised with Christ, set your hearts on things above, where Christ is, seated at the right hand of God. [2] Set your minds on things above, not on earthly things.

Colossians 3:1-2

We can't solve this with positive thinking, self-help, or willpower. Paul tells the Colossians that before they received Jesus, their problem wasn't a lack of spirituality or religious effort.

They were enemies of God in their minds because of their evil behavior.

This explains why Paul doesn't say, "Try your best to avoid those things if you can." There is nothing casual about his response.

He says, "Put them to death."

The clear implication is this: Either we put these desires to death, or eventually they'll do the same to us. The longer you walk with God, the more you realize this is not a joke.

But Paul doesn't stop with evil desires. Through the leading of the Holy Spirit, Paul goes further into the arena of our thoughts, challenging us to rid ourselves of anger, rage, malice, slander, and filthy language. None of these lead to a healthy thought life.

Setting our minds above is not an instruction to literally look up. It's all about what we focus on.

In this metaphor, to look down is to fixate on the problems of this world. This is easy to do. Our culture trains us to hyper-focus on fear and the wide range of potential problems we could face.

Fear is the most powerful human motivator. It influences how people think, how people talk, and what people do with their money.

This is not to deny the fact we live in a fallen world. We see the wickedness, corruption, brokenness, and all the other effects of sin around us.

Put to death, therefore, whatever belongs to your earthly nature: sexual immorality, impurity, lust, evil desires and greed, which is idolatry.

Colossians 3:5

But now you must also rid yourselves of all such things as these: anger, rage, malice, slander, and filthy language from your lips.

Colossians 3:8

TO FIND YOUR PURPOSE... YOU HAVE TO LOOK DEEPER INTO JESUS.

But when we focus on these things, it can be very difficult to find hope for the future and the promise of a better life.

To set our minds above is to look to our resurrected Jesus, who defeated sin, death, and all the forces of darkness. When we remember Him, we remember our true lives are hidden in Him, and only through Him can we discover what we're longing for.

Jesus is more than our Savior and our Lord—He is our life. It's only found in Him.

In order to find your purpose, you don't look deeper into yourself. You have to look deeper into Jesus.

CONTEXT

In the ancient world, idolatry was primarily viewed as an effective way to manipulate some material advantage from the gods. Worshiping gods was a means to an end—an attempt to outsmart them or to feign allegiance long enough to produce some divine wish or favor.

Dancing and shouting for hours, depriving yourself of food, and enduring suffering or intense pain were all encouraged. Then, perhaps, the pagan gods would smile on you and grant you your wish.

Because they had been culturally conditioned to live this way, the people of Israel would apply this approach to observing the laws and worshiping the God of the Bible.

That was never His plan. He's not fickle. He doesn't inconsistently reward extreme acts of self-righteousness.

Because God genuinely loves people and cares for their well-being, His goal was something much greater than granting wishes like a cosmic genie. He did not want to relate to His people through manipulation.

God wants our hearts. He wants a genuine and authentic relationship with us.

Relating to God in this way required their minds to be renewed and their thoughts to be transformed.

This is what Paul means when he reminds them that they've died to this old way of thinking and their lives are now hidden in Christ. This mentality is the old self that must be set aside in order for the new self to be put on.

And this new self is not a manipulative attempt to gain divine advantages—it is being completely content in the purpose and person of Christ.

Colossians 3:1-10

1 Since, then, you have been raised with Christ,
set your hearts on things above, where Christ is,
seated at the right hand of God. 2 Set your minds on
things above, not on earthly things. 3 For you died,
and your life is now hidden with Christ in God.
4 When Christ, who is your life, appears, then you
also will appear with him in glory.

5 Put to death, therefore, whatever belongs to your
earthly nature: sexual immorality, impurity, lust,
evil desires and greed, which is idolatry. 6 Because
of these, the wrath of God is coming. 7 You used
to walk in these ways, in the life you once lived.
8 But now you must also rid yourselves of all such
things as these: anger, rage, malice, slander, and
filthy language from your lips.

9 Do not lie to each other, since you have taken off
your old self with its practices 10 and have put on
the new self, which is being renewed in knowledge
in the image of its Creator.

WHAT DOES THIS MEAN FOR US?

This new way of thinking is more than just positive thoughts or personal willpower. Paul is not advocating extreme discipline in order to improve our spiritual standing. This far exceeds a makeover or a spiritual improvement project.

He employs Jesus' language of death and new birth. He could not be more direct. He says, "You died, and your life is now hidden in God."

If you want to find your new life, don't listen when culture tells you to look inside yourself. Your heart, your passions, your desires, and your truth cannot lead you to your new life.

The only place you can find it is hidden in Christ. To be hidden means it's not obvious. It will take some time. You're going to have to look for it.

Remember, Colossians 2:13 says that when we were dead in our sins, God made us alive in Christ. Because of what Jesus did for us on the cross, He forgave our sins and made us right with Him.

> When you were dead in your sins and in the uncircumcision of your flesh, God made you alive with Christ. He forgave us all our sins.
>
> **Colossians 2:13**

This should strengthen our faith. Because God loved us so much, He didn't spare His Son, but offered Him on our behalf so we could be made right with Him.

> He who did not spare his own Son, but gave him up for us all—how will he not also, along with him, graciously give us all things?
>
> **Romans 8:32**

There is no greater demonstration of love God could ever give. We don't have to worry or be afraid that He's holding out on us or looking for a reason to punish us.

He has given us everything we need for life and godliness. He will meet all of our needs according to His riches and glory.

> And my God will meet all your needs according to the riches of his glory in Christ Jesus.
>
> **Philippians 4:19**

This is who God is. His character and nature should shape all of our thoughts.

How different would our lives be if every thought we entertained was put through the filter of God's amazing love for us?

In Romans 12:2, Paul says to avoid conforming to the thoughts and attitudes (the pattern) of this world, and instead be transformed by the renewing of our minds.

> Do not conform to the pattern of this world, but be transformed by the renewing of your mind. Then you will be able to test and approve what God's will is—his good, pleasing and perfect will.
>
> **Romans 12:2**

A renewed mind overflows with thanksgiving and gratitude.

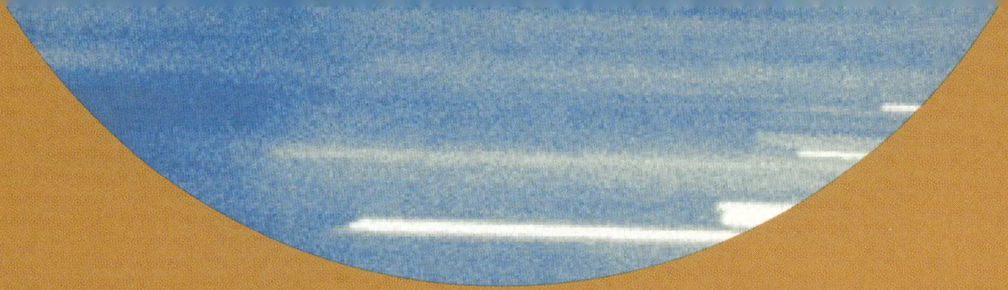

What Do I Do with This?

We don't spontaneously fall into a new way of thinking.

No one accidentally renews their minds. It requires intentional steps.

ONE: DON'T LET FEAR, ANXIETY, AND WORRY DOMINATE YOUR THOUGHTS.

Stop fixating on all of the latest problems being messaged to you through your phone. Remember the supremacy of Christ. Jesus has first place in everything. He wins. And if we're in Him, we win too.

TWO: TAKE NEGATIVE THOUGHTS CAPTIVE BEFORE THEY LEAD TO TEMPTATIONS OR ACTIONS.

Practically, this means fleshly desires, unrighteous appetites, and toxic emotions. None of us are immune from these things. We have to build disciplines that demonstrate our commitment to personal holiness.

We can't stop these thoughts from coming, but we can refuse to let them stay. It's like the difference between a bird that flies by your head and a bird that builds a nest. One leaves quickly, while the other one makes a home.

THREE: MEMORIZE, MEDITATE ON, AND CONFESS GOD'S WORD.

The only way for us to become the person God created us to be is to think and confess (say aloud) what He says about us.

No one puts together a puzzle without looking at the finished picture of what it's supposed to look like. In the same way, our thinking and our character are designed to look like God.

We can only make progress when we know God's character and nature.

Discussion

Read Colossians 3:1-10: [1] Since, then, you have been raised with Christ, set your hearts on things above,
where Christ is, seated at the right hand of God. [2] Set your minds on things above, not on earthly things. [3] For
you died, and your life is now hidden with Christ in God. [4] When Christ, who is your life, appears, then you also
will appear with him in glory.

[5] Put to death, therefore, whatever belongs to your earthly nature: sexual immorality, impurity, lust, evil desires
and greed, which is idolatry. [6] Because of these, the wrath of God is coming. [7] You used to walk in these ways,
in the life you once lived. [8] But now you must also rid yourselves of all such things as these: anger, rage, malice,
slander, and filthy language from your lips.

[9] Do not lie to each other, since you have taken off your old self with its practices [10] and have put on the new
self, which is being renewed in knowledge in the image of its Creator.

1. **Read verse 2. What does it mean to "set your mind on things above"? Why is this important?**

2. **Read verse 3. Paul says that your new life is "hidden with Christ in God." What do you have to do to find something that's hidden? How does this apply to the life God has for you?**

3. **Read verses 5-9. What does it mean to put to death your old self?**

4. Are there any areas that belong to your "earthly nature" that you still struggle with? What are they?

5. Why are the things that belong to our "earthly nature" so difficult to put to death?

6. Read verse 10. What does it mean to put on your new self?

7. Review the three application points on pages 66-67. Which of these points stands out to you the most today, and why?

1. Don't let fear, anxiety, and worry dominate your thoughts.
2. Take negative thoughts captive before they lead to temptations or actions.
3. Memorize, meditate on, and confess God's Word.

Questions

Application

Take a moment to examine your life.

What areas need to change, whether in your thoughts, actions, words, or attitudes?

What does God want you to do about these areas?

Prayer

Jesus, I know ***Life on Purpose*** requires me to align my thoughts with Your Word. Help me to capture the anxiety, fear, worry, and toxic thoughts that try to fill my mind. Help my mind and my thoughts to be filled with Your truth and Your promises. In Jesus' name, Amen.

Week Three

03.

YOUR *RELATIONSHIPS*

THEME VERSE

Therefore, as God's chosen people, holy and dearly loved, clothe yourselves with compassion, kindness, humility, gentleness and patience.

Colossians 3:12

KEY TRUTH

Life on Purpose promotes healthy relationships.

PASSAGE

Colossians 3:12-14

CONCEPT

IT *may sound cliché*, BUT IN THE END, *life is* ALL ABOUT *how we relate* TO OTHERS.

We are hard-wired for relationships.

And although we are more technologically connected than any era in history, we are also experiencing an epidemic of loneliness.

This phenomenon is often described as "crowded loneliness"—*I'm around people all day long but I feel like no one sees me, truly knows me, or cares about me.*

Prolonged seasons of life in this mentality are both miserable and, eventually, life-threatening. Multiple times over the last

!

We cannot experience *Life on Purpose* without prioritizing healthy relationships.

few years, the surgeon general of the United States has emphasized how dangerous this threat is to our well-being as a nation.

Unfortunately, one of the most common responses to this condition also happens to be one of its primary causes.

Selfishness.

Human beings have always been selfish, but we've never culturally rewarded this posture the way we do now.

The life we've been created to live does not work this way.

We cannot experience *Life on Purpose* without prioritizing healthy relationships.

Because relationships have multiple parts, we cannot control them. We can only do our part.

We have to start from a posture that aspires to love and serve the people in our lives the way God has loved and served us.

Colossians 3:12 challenges us to be compassionate, kind, humble, gentle, and patient. Not because it comes easy to us or we feel like it, but because we've been chosen and loved by God, included in His family, and called to love others the way He's loved us.

Therefore, as God's chosen people, holy and dearly loved, clothe yourselves with compassion, kindness, humility, gentleness and patience.

Colossians 3:12

✦ ✦ ✦

Our culture promotes extreme individualism because it's a successful marketing approach whether you're selling shoes or smartphones.

None of us have to be taught to put ourselves first—even at the expense of others. It's human nature.

If you're worried about what someone else is thinking about you, don't worry, they're not. They're too busy thinking about themselves.

It's a terrible way to build relationships.

We all know what it's like to be around people whose attitude and demeanor are completely dependent upon them getting their way wherever they go and whatever they do.

It's exhausting. Most people stuff their emotions so they distance themselves from these people the best they can to avoid the drama.

The smaller group, who are more inclined to confront this behavior, usually discover these encounters only give selfish people another reason to stir up drama and make it about themselves.

John Wooden, one of the greatest coaches in history, once said, "Happiness begins where selfishness ends."

The other major downside to selfishness is how quickly it

divides us. People who are consumed with themselves are keenly aware of all the ways others are different from them.

We've lost the ability to agree to disagree in maturity. While our culture preaches "tolerance," in reality, the actual message is anyone who fails to condone all of your views or beliefs is hostile and oppressing you.

Outside of loneliness, polarization is one of our greatest cultural challenges. It fractures homes, offices, schools, neighborhoods, cities, and nations.

CONTEXT

Remember, one of the primary reasons the Holy Spirit inspired Paul to write to the people of Colossae was in response to the dangerous philosophies and teachings creeping into the church.

The primary controversy centered on dividing people into true and false believers based on their observance of religious laws instead of their faith and commitment to Jesus.

Religious achievement makes people feel spiritual and better than their neighbors. It's selfish, divisive, and erodes trust.

Our pride craves reasons to feel superior to others.

Human nature is tribal. We divide the world into good people and bad people. The cool table isn't just a thing in middle school.

OUR ONLY HOPE FOR HEALTHY RELATIONSHIPS IS JESUS.

Paul says we have to put these attitudes to death. They're part of the old self. He said to stop seeing ourselves as Jews and Gentiles, circumcised and uncircumcised, slave or free, or any other way we divide ourselves.

These people lived on the other side of the planet thousands of years ago, but basic human tendencies and behavior have not changed.

The hope for our relationships is not chemistry or shared interests. We have different backgrounds, different experiences, and different stories.

Our only hope for healthy relationships is Jesus.

He is ALL, and when He's in ALL, we can love and serve each other.

There is neither Jew nor Gentile, neither slave nor free, nor is there male and female, for you are all one in Christ Jesus.

Galatians 3:28

Colossians 3:12-14

12 Therefore, as God's chosen people, holy
and dearly loved, clothe yourselves with
compassion, kindness, humility, gentleness
and patience. 13 Bear with each other and
forgive one another if any of you has a
grievance against someone. Forgive as the
Lord forgave you. 14 And over all these virtues
put on love, which binds them all together in
perfect unity.

WHAT DOES THIS MEAN FOR US?

The Bible promotes a completely different view of relationships.

When Paul starts a lengthy section to the Colossians on healthy relationships, he starts by encouraging them to see themselves as part of God's chosen people, holy and dearly loved.

What does this mean?

We find security, significance, and meaning not based on our accomplishments, the goals we've achieved, or our personal passions.

***Life on Purpose*, the life we've been created to live, is found in seeing ourselves fundamentally as chosen by God to be part of His family.**

Both culture and our fallen nature start with: *What's in it for me?* Healthy relationships start with: *It's not about me.*

To be holy is to be set apart; you don't think or live like everybody else. You have enough self-awareness to recognize the difference between what your flesh and the culture tell you versus what God says.

Most people think holiness is a standard we strive for so God will love us. We can never hit that target. It makes us critical of everyone else and leaves us exhausted and afraid.

We only live holy *after* we know how much God loved us when we were His enemies, separated from God, and dead in our sin.

We relate to others from God's love and approval, not in order to win it from Him with our perfect performance.

Paul challenges us to clothe ourselves with compassion, kindness, humility, gentleness, and patience.

This is an important metaphor.

You have to make the choice to put your clothes on. It's an intentional act we do every morning, whether we feel like it or not. It's what we want others to see when they look at us.

These attributes are more than a list. They're a picture of the culture of relationships we should aspire to cultivate in every context of our lives.

We have no control over how others treat us, but we're the only ones responsible for whether or not we're compassionate, kind, humble, gentle, and patient.

We don't do those things for other people when and if they earn it. That's what self-righteous, religious people do.

We do those things because that's how God has called us to live and that's how He treated us before we ever did anything to earn or deserve it.

The only way we'll ever consistently have the ability to forgive others is because we know God has forgiven us.

It's not even about us—it's Christ in us.

This is more than lip service. This is more than a religious platitude.

And the only lasting motivation to consistently live this way is love. Not the love the world talks about. Not some fleeting, heartfelt feeling.

When the Bible talks about love, it's talking about something much more valuable. Much more costly.

In Romans 5:8, Paul reminds us that God demonstrated His love for us in that while we were sinners, Christ died for us. He didn't just feel love, He demonstrated it.

But God demonstrates his own love for us in this: While we were still sinners, Christ died for us.

Romans 5:8

1 John 3:16 says, "This is how we know what love is: Jesus Christ laid down his life for us. And we ought to lay down our lives for our brothers and sisters."

If we're going to have healthy relationships, we need this kind of love. We need the ability to give this kind of love. And there's only one place to get it. It doesn't come from the way the people in your life treat you.

It comes from a perfect God who demonstrated His love for you while you were dead in sin.

Every good gift in your life has come from Him.

He has given you everything you need for life and godliness. He will never leave you or forsake you. He will never stop loving you.

Every good and perfect gift is from above, coming down from the Father of the heavenly lights, who does not change like shifting shadows.

James 1:17

"Be strong and courageous. Do not be afraid or terrified because of them, for the Lord your God goes with you; he will never leave you nor forsake you."

Deuteronomy 31:6

What Do I Do with This?

You can't give what you don't have.

ONE: REGULARLY RECEIVE THIS LOVE FROM GOD.

This comes from spending time with Him. It could be as simple as a few moments each morning reading your Bible, praying, and worshiping.

TWO: CLOTHE YOURSELF WITH GOD'S HEART FOR PEOPLE.

You intentionally put these attitudes (compassion, kindness, humility, gentleness, and patience) on each morning whether you feel like it or not. Not because people have earned it. And not because you always do the right thing in all your relationships. But you're intentional to make this the goal in how you want to treat people.

THREE: ASK GOD TO SHOW YOU, "WHAT DOES IT LOOK LIKE FOR ME TO LOVE THIS PERSON IN THIS SITUATION?"

The great thing about this approach is it applies whether it's your spouse, one of your kids, a friend, a neighbor, a roommate, a parent, a sibling, a coworker . . . or anyone else in your life.

Discussion

Read Colossians 3:12-14: [12] Therefore, as God's chosen people, holy and dearly loved, clothe yourselves with compassion, kindness, humility, gentleness and patience. [13] Bear with each other and forgive one another if any of you has a grievance against someone. Forgive as the Lord forgave you. [14] And over all these virtues put on love, which binds them all together in perfect unity.

1. One of the primary causes of loneliness in the world is selfishness. Do you agree or disagree with this statement? Explain.

2. How does our culture encourage and even reward selfishness?

3. Read verse 12. Why does Paul use the illustration of clothing yourself in this verse?

4. What does Paul tell us to clothe ourselves with? Which of the attributes in verse 12 do you need to grow in the most? Explain.

5. Read verses 13-14. Why is forgiveness important for unity? Why is forgiveness so difficult sometimes?

6. What's the right motivation for treating others right? Why is this important?

7. How can we continually receive God's love in order to love others?

Questions

Application

Take a moment to think through your relationships.

Who is someone you need to show God's love?

What does it look like for you to love this person in this situation?

Prayer

Jesus, I believe ***Life on Purpose*** promotes healthy relationships in every area of my life. Help me to offer Your compassion, kindness, humility, gentleness, and patience to others. I know I can't control their actions, but my prayer is to love them the way You have loved me. In Your name, Amen.

Week Four

04.

YOUR *PEACE*

THEME VERSE

Let the peace of Christ rule in your hearts, since as members of one body you were called to peace. And be thankful.

Colossians 3:15

KEY TRUTH

Life on Purpose prioritizes peace over our emotions and desires.

PASSAGE

Colossians 3:15-17

CONCEPT

WHAT WOULD YOU ***trade for peace?*** IF YOU'RE A PARENT OF SMALL CHILDREN, THERE'S ***nothing like those moments*** RIGHT AFTER THE KIDS FINALLY GO DOWN FOR THE NIGHT. ***The house seems almost too quiet.***

You love those little bundles of energy, but those first few moments for yourself are incredible.

You think to yourself, *Finally . . . a little peace and quiet.*

Peace is more than the absence of problems—it's the sense that everything is right in the world.

!

We can live ***Life on Purpose*** when peace rules in our hearts.

If you've been in a busy season at work where it feels like there's always another deadline, you're staying late or bringing work home every night, and the list of projects never seems to end… a couple days off can help.

But what you really need is peace.

More than a feeling, it's the sense that all your hard work is paying off. You experience the fulfillment and significance that's only found by contributing your part to something truly meaningful.

Jesus wants us to have this peace. And not only to have it, but to let it rule over our thoughts and our emotions. He's called us to live this way. But we have to receive it.

Let the peace of Christ rule in your hearts, since as members of one body you were called to peace. And be thankful.

Colossians 3:15

Colossians 3:15 tells us to let the peace of Christ rule in our hearts—since we were called as members of one body to peace—and to be thankful.

We can live *Life on Purpose* when peace rules in our hearts.

For to us a child is born, to us a son is given, and the government will be on his shoulders. And he will be called Wonderful Counselor, Mighty God, Everlasting Father, Prince of Peace.

Isaiah 9:6

The Bible calls Jesus the Prince of Peace, which means He is the authority on the subject.

It comes from Him. His version of peace isn't temporary or insignificant.

The Hebrew word for peace, "shalom," is often used as a greeting and a blessing. But it's more than a cultural pleasantry. It's a constant acknowledgment that this is what we all want.

Jesus promised to give us His peace. A peace that cannot be taken away.

When you've endured prolonged conflicts in your family, whether between siblings, spouses, parents and teens, parents and adult children, or in-laws (and outlaws), you would love reconciliation.

But after a certain point, you'd be willing to settle for a ceasefire during family dinners or a birthday party.

Less drama. Less stress. Less conflict.

You wonder, *Is this even possible?* Left to our own ability to control situations, the answer is no.

We're driven people. We have goals and ambitions. But what we really need is the peace of God. This peace Jesus came to bring.

The problem is, most of us don't know where to find it or how it works. That's why we end up trying to work, control, or manipulate our way into this kind of peace. We think we can achieve, experience, or accomplish peace by hitting goals and dreams we set for ourselves.

It doesn't work. We end up more frustrated and anxious.

"Peace I leave with you; my peace I give you. I do not give to you as the world gives. Do not let your hearts be troubled and do not be afraid."

John 14:27

But as we continue to give these relationships to Jesus, He brings His peace. This doesn't mean we won't have future challenges, but it definitely changes our ability to experience His peace.

And at the deepest level, this peace changes the quality of our lives.

CONTEXT

The people of Colossae lived halfway around the world, thousands of years ago, but these people are a lot like us.

They were experiencing relational challenges and conflict because of their differences. Divisive people were separating them into combative groups, argumentative tribes, "in groups" and "out groups" on the basis of opinions and customs that had nothing to do with God or His Kingdom.

Sound familiar?

If we want peace in our homes, in our church, in our workplace, in our children's schools, in our friend groups, we have to understand where it comes from. And we have to understand the attitudes and beliefs that disrupt our peace.

What would you be willing to trade for peace?

- Your personal preferences?
- Your comfort?
- Your right to be offended and bitter?
- Your desire to always be right or look smart?
- A title, a promotion, or goals?

Jesus gave up all of these things and more to give you His peace.

What is His peace worth to you?

Paul says we must let the peace of Christ *rule* in our hearts—to "rule" is to have the highest place. Remember, the second half of the first chapter in Colossians is about how Jesus is unlike anyone else. He is supreme, He has first place in everything. He holds everything together, and all things were made by Him and for Him.

And for those of us in Him, we have been called to peace. In other words, it's not optional. It's the intended purpose. It's the desired outcome.

We all want peace because it's what we've been created for.

And we can't make it on our own.

Colossians 3:15-17

15 Let the peace of Christ rule in your hearts,
since as members of one body you were
called to peace. And be thankful.
16 Let the message of Christ dwell among
you richly as you teach and admonish one
another with all wisdom through psalms,
hymns, and songs from the Spirit, singing to
God with gratitude in your hearts.
17 And whatever you do, whether in word or
deed, do it all in the name of the Lord Jesus,
giving thanks to God the Father through him.

WHAT DOES THIS MEAN FOR US?

Peace is not a mysterious add-on for a few special people. Remember, Jesus promised to give us His peace.

He said He doesn't give like the world gives, so when we have His peace our hearts don't need to be troubled and we don't need to be afraid. He also said the only place to find this peace is in Him.

In another one of Paul's letters, he tells a group of believers not to worry about anything, but in everything, to make their requests known to God with thanksgiving.

Notice how he connects thanksgiving to peace again, just like he does in this letter.

Paul said that when we do this, the peace of God, which transcends our understanding, will guard our hearts and our minds in Christ Jesus.

[6] Do not be anxious about anything, but in every situation, by prayer and petition, with thanksgiving, present your requests to God. [7] And the peace of God, which transcends all understanding, will guard your hearts and your minds in Christ Jesus.

Philippians 4:6-7

In a world that says, "Trust your heart," "Follow your heart," "Listen to your heart," and "The heart wants what the heart wants," the Bible continually reminds us to *guard* our hearts.

As one of the great hymns reminds us, our hearts are prone to wander.[3]

Jesus tells us not to let our hearts be troubled because that's the direction they move. They're not neutral—they're easily troubled, distracted, confused, and deceived.

Jeremiah 17:9a says: "The heart is deceitful above all things." Proverbs 4:23b cautions: "Guard your heart, for everything you do flows from it."

A simple way to guard our hearts is to continually be thankful. Hearts that are selfish and greedy are never satisfied. They are incapable of enjoying what God has generously provided.

Instead, Jesus tells us to follow His example and to learn from Him because He is humble in His heart. A humble heart leads to rest in our souls.

"Take my yoke upon you and learn from me, for I am gentle and humble in heart, and you will find rest for your souls."

Matthew 11:29

What a great description of peace!

You might think, *But I don't feel grateful and I don't want to be fake.* Remember, we lead our hearts, we don't let our hearts lead us.

[3] "Come, Thou Fount of Every Blessing," is one of the most well-known and loved hymns of all time—written in 1758 by Robert Robinson at just 22 years old.

GRATITUDE IS A CHOICE.

Gratitude is a choice.

Jesus said every good thing we experience in life is a gift from our loving Father. No matter what circumstances we're facing, all of us can find multiple things each day we can be grateful for when we take the time to look and consider all of God's goodness toward us.

Perhaps the best way to live this out is to teach and encourage others with Scripture and worship songs. Not out of religious duty but from a heart filled with gratitude and thanksgiving.

Maybe you've never considered this, but authentic worship and singing to God with a grateful heart is something you can do on your own. It's certainly powerful when we gather together in worship, but if we want this kind of peace, we can build it into our daily lives and make it a consistent part of our routine.

If you say, "I'm not musical," or, "I don't sing well," you're not alone in those assessments. But that's not what truly matters.

It's about your heart far more than your voice. It's about turning your heart, your affections, and your intentions toward God on a regular basis.

A bright side to all of our technology is the ease with which we can find and enjoy worship music.

When we're regularly experiencing the peace of God with a

grateful heart, we're able to connect whatever we're doing with our relationship with Jesus. We can do it for Him, whether it's serving our family, keeping a great attitude at work, loving our neighbors, or keeping our hearts right.

What Do I Do with This?

There are several basic things we can do to grow in this area.

ONE: LET PEACE RULE IN YOUR HEART.

To rule is to be in charge. Most days this means you have to remind your heart not to be afraid or pursue unrighteous desires, but instead to line up with God and His Word.

In order to receive the peace Jesus wants to give us, we also have to receive His authority. We don't get one without the other.

TWO: CULTIVATE GRATITUDE— BE THANKFUL.

Take a moment every day to tell God about something specific you're grateful for. You can tell Him out loud, you can write it down, you can keep a journal. Any of these options will build the habit of focusing on God's goodness instead of on your struggles or needs.

THREE: DEVELOP A ROUTINE OF PERSONAL WORSHIP.

You could put on your headphones and listen to a song while you're having your first cup of coffee. You could play worship music while you're getting dressed. Instead of a podcast, talking on the phone, or listening to the radio, you could make your daily commute a time for you and God.

However you choose to do it, this simple practice will drastically increase the measure of God's peace you experience in your daily life.

Discussion

Read Colossians 3:15-17: [15] Let the peace of Christ rule in your hearts, since as members of one body you were called to peace. And be thankful. [16] Let the message of Christ dwell among you richly as you teach and admonish one another with all wisdom through psalms, hymns, and songs from the Spirit, singing to God with gratitude in your hearts. [17] And whatever you do, whether in word or deed, do it all in the name of the Lord Jesus, giving thanks to God the Father through him.

1. **How would you describe biblical peace after reading this chapter?**

2. **Read Colossians 3:15 again. Why would Paul tell us to let the peace of Christ rule in our hearts? What does the word "rule" imply?**

3. **What are some of the wrong places or ways we look for peace?**

4. **Colossians 3:15-17 mentions the idea of thankfulness and gratitude three times. The Bible often connects thankfulness and gratitude with peace. Why?**

5. How do our hearts often lead us away from peace, and what's the solution?

6. Take a moment to list five things you are grateful for. What are the first five things that come to mind? Then list five additional, less obvious things you are grateful for.

7. How did making the list in Question 6 make you feel? What did it produce in you? And what is God trying to show you through this exercise?

8. How does authentic worship help cultivate gratitude and peace?

9. How often do you spend time worshiping God? How can you grow in this area?

Questions

Application

Page 100 asks the question: What would you be willing to trade for peace?

Is there anything in your life you are currently trading for peace? What is it?

What does God want you to do about it?

Prayer

Jesus, I know ***Life on Purpose*** is filled with Your peace. I put Your peace above my desires and emotions. I receive it by faith, and I know nothing can take it from me. In Your name I pray, Amen.

Week Five

05.

YOUR *FAMILY*

THEME VERSE

And whatever you do, whether in word or deed, do it all in the name of the Lord Jesus, giving thanks to God the Father through him.

Colossians 3:17

KEY TRUTH

Life on Purpose follows God's plan for our families.

PASSAGE

Colossians 3:18-21

CONCEPT

THERE IS ***nothing*** IN LIFE ***quite like family.***

Every human being comes into the world in a family THEY DON'T GET TO CHOOSE. ***The highs can be so high,*** AND THE LOWS CAN BE ***unimaginably low.***

For good and for bad, our families shape, mold, and influence who we become.

Perhaps our culture has never had more opinions about family than today. You can find nearly every possible perspective and opinion about this subject through social media, the internet, books, podcasts, television, and movies.

!

Life on Purpose follows God's plan for our families.

And whatever new forms of media are created in the future, it won't take long for people to talk about family on those as well.

No matter how hard we try, we can't get away from family. It's foundational to who we are as people. Schools, workplaces, hobby groups, and even sports fans use family language to describe their relationships.

Today our culture treats family like it treats most things—truth, spirituality, purpose, and meaning—claiming it can be whatever you want it to be, as long as you don't offend someone else.

Part of being a family is taking family pictures. Everyone who has participated in this knows how difficult it can be. It's a surefire way to test the relational health of your family! But it's a helpful analogy:

Every member of the family moves in the direction of the picture they have in their minds of what they want the family to be.

This becomes especially challenging when we're not moving toward the same picture.

These differences cause so many of the misunderstandings, challenges, and pain in our families. The problem is not that we don't care—we care so much. But we don't know how to get everyone moving in the same direction.

***Life on Purpose* follows God's plan for our families.**

Without a plan, we get in trouble. We've all been there.

Every family is a collection of humans with unique preferences, desires, expectations, and wants and needs. Trying to get them to agree on anything (i.e. what to eat, what to watch) can feel impossible.

The only way it works is for the whole family to follow one plan—not Dad's, Mom's, or the kids' . . . but God's plan.

In Colossians 3, right before Paul gets really specific and laser-focused toward each member of the family, he gives a general principle for how families should treat each other.

He basically says, whatever you do or say with your family, do it all in the name of Jesus while you're giving thanks to the Father.

It's brilliant because it's simple. But it requires commitment.

Your wife does the thing you asked her not to do but instead of saying, "I told you so," you offer grace.

That's doing it for Jesus.

Your husband is short with you and says something that hurts your feelings, but instead of hurting him back you find a way to encourage him.

That's doing it for Jesus.

And whatever you do, whether in word or deed, do it all in the name of the Lord Jesus, giving thanks to God the Father through him.

Colossians 3:17

Your parents are having a hard time at work and forget something you really need for a school project. Instead of getting upset, you thank them for all the ways they love and serve you.

That's doing it for Jesus.

✦✦✦

Family is God's idea.

It's how He builds. Out of all the terms He could have chosen to describe Himself, He chose Father. When we needed a Savior, He sent more than a warrior, a champion, a hero, or a king. He sent His Son.

> See what great love the Father has lavished on us, that we should be called children of God! And that is what we are!
>
> **1 John 3:1a**

He doesn't just invite us into His Kingdom. He doesn't just call us citizens of heaven.

> For God so loved the world that he gave his one and only Son, that whoever believes in him shall not perish but have eternal life.
>
> **John 3:16**

He doesn't just forgive our sins. He takes us into His family and calls us His sons and daughters.

No one cares more about family than God.

The Bible says every family on earth gets their name from Him. He sees your family. He cares for it more than you do.

> 14 For this reason I kneel before the Father, 15 from whom every family in heaven and on earth derives its name.
>
> **Ephesians 3:14-15**

He wants to bless your family. But He reserves His blessing for His pattern and His picture.

If we want God's blessing on our families, we have to follow His plan.

CONTEXT

Colossians 3:18-21 is an example of a New Testament "household code."

We can find similar passages describing the relationship between husbands and wives in Ephesians 5:21-33 and 1 Peter 3:1-7, children and fathers in Ephesians 6:1-4, and extended family in 1 Timothy 5:1-16.

Household codes date back to at least the time of Aristotle, and they were regularly used by both Greek and Roman philosophers to describe cultural standards for a stable home in order to ensure the stability of civilization.

However, in the Greek and Roman codes, only the male head of the household was addressed. In Rome, the role of wives was to unquestionably obey the commands of the man, who was afforded legal rights no one else in the family was granted. Children were the legal property of the man.

In the New Testament, both parties (wife and husband, child and parent, servant and master) are addressed, and in most cases, the subordinate figure is addressed first. The Bible views husbands and wives, and parents and children, as having equal value before God, but different roles and responsibilities.

This was in stark contrast to the rest of the culture.

It's also helpful to remember the ancient world was much less individualistic and more communal. A household was not made up of individuals who prioritized personal expression and autonomy. These were groups whose lives were inextricably connected—often beyond blood relatives or kin to include everyone who lived in the home.

In keeping with a major theme in Scripture, as the head of the household, the man was expected to lead, not through commands and position but through loving service.

Colossians 3:18-21

18 Wives, submit yourselves to your husbands,
as is fitting in the Lord.
19 Husbands, love your wives and do not be
harsh with them.
20 Children, obey your parents in everything,
for this pleases the Lord.
21 Fathers, do not embitter your children, or
they will become discouraged.

WHAT DOES THIS MEAN FOR US?

There's a whole lot to unpack in these four simple verses.

First, we need to remember the passage immediately preceding these verses. Paul's statement leading into this family discussion is important: Whatever you do, do it all in the name of the Lord Jesus, giving thanks to God the Father through Him (Colossians 3:17). If we are genuinely in Christ, it should be easily recognizable through the way we treat others.

And the first place this starts is in our homes.

It takes more than a Christian symbol or Scripture hanging on the wall to make a Christian home. A Bible on the coffee table or nightstand won't do it either. All of those can be meaningful, but it's more than décor.

You can sense peace in a Christian home because of how they

love and serve each other, not because each member has earned it, but because of their obedience to Jesus.

Second, remember the ancient cultural norms surrounding the family. Women were not viewed as equals. Listing the wife first in this passage would not have signaled pointing a finger in blame at her to the original audience. It would have signaled inclusion and equality. It would have emphasized the importance of her contribution and role.

When a wife submits to her husband out of obedience to the Lord, she is not taking a lesser, subservient role. In Genesis when God said man needed a helper, the word used there is the same word used to describe the Holy Spirit. That's how God talks about how the Spirit loves and serves the Father and the Son!

So, when a woman loves and serves her husband with this attitude, she's following God's pattern and can therefore expect God's blessing.

Third, not only does the passage challenge husbands to love their wives, it goes the extra mile to remind them not to be harsh. You can be right with the wrong attitude. You can say the right thing with an unkind tone.

This is less than God's best. It's less than the good life. It's a lower standard than the life we were created to live. A husband who is rooted in Christ speaks life to his wife, encourages her, challenges her, listens to her, and is constantly mindful of his tone.

The Lord God said, "It is not good for the man to be alone. I will make a helper suitable for him."

Genesis 2:18

This doesn't mean he's perfect, but it does mean he understands that how he treats his wife is a clear reflection of how he loves God.

God created the marriage relationship as a key ingredient in the process of our sanctification (how He makes us more like Him).[4]

When husbands and wives make this the standard for their relationship, both grow into a better version of who God created them to be. They experience more of His purpose and blessing in their lives.

Fourth, children are challenged to obey their parents because it pleases the Lord. This does not place obedience to our parents above obedience to God but instead assumes a general posture of love and honor that isn't dependent upon the worthiness of our parents but on the worthiness of God.

Ephesians 6 explains this is the first command that has a promise attached to it: God's blessing of a good, long life. Notice there is no expiration date on this command. Adult children are still under this challenge... and still eligible for God's blessing.

[1] Children, obey your parents in the Lord, for this is right. [2] "Honor your father and mother"—which is the first commandment with a promise— [3] "so that it may go well with you and that you may enjoy long life on the earth."

Ephesians 6:1-3

Finally, in keeping with the previous direction, fathers are cautioned not to embitter their children because it will cause them to be discouraged. Some dads are aggressive, constantly disappointed with their children, and slow to offer loving encouragement. Other dads are disengaged, preoccupied with other things, and allow their kids to do whatever they want.

[4] This does NOT mean that single people are lacking or unable to grow into the person God created them to be. God can and does use any relationship to sanctify us. The more important issue is the willingness of the person to grow in their walk with God through the way they love and treat others.

Both approaches are damaging. The words of a father have a massive impact on their children, and most of us project our earliest understandings of God as an extension of our relationship with our earthly fathers.

However, God can heal, restore, and reach us no matter what our relationship with our earthly father is like. His love and goodness have no limits.

It's worth noticing that two of the four commands in this brief passage are directed at the man of the home. This is not a reflection of a higher worth or value, but it is a window into his importance in setting the tone and creating an environment of health and peace in the home.

What Do I Do with This?

Remember, family is God's idea. And in order to get God's blessing, we have to follow God's plan.

ONE: SET GOD UP AS THE HEAD OF THE HOUSEHOLD.

Husbands love wives not because they've earned it but because of their love for Jesus. Wives serve their husbands because of the goodness and faithfulness of God. Parents disciple their children because they believe God has given them as a gift.

This is covenant language—*I promise to do this out of my love for God.* Too often families try to operate based on contract language—*if you do this, I'll do that.* Eventually, it breaks down because no one

Children are a gift from the Lord; they are a reward from him.

Psalm 127:3 (NLT)

sees our weaknesses more than the people we live with every day. We're not perfect, and we see it in each other.

When every member of the family makes it their goal to love and honor God instead of competing with each other and keeping score, we get to encourage each other to become a better version of who God created us to be.

TWO: BE QUICK TO FORGIVE AND HARD TO OFFEND.

Most families are really good at holding grudges. We think it will protect us from getting hurt in the future or make us feel better when we're upset.

It doesn't work.

The healthiest families love and forgive each other. Not because they deserve it or have earned forgiveness, but because they understand God has forgiven them. They don't keep score. They don't remember all the things they've done to each other.

And they don't wait for the other person—they're willing to go first. The first to say they're sorry. The first to make it right. The first to offer loving encouragement. The first to pray God's blessing over the other members of their family.

This doesn't mean they overlook or ignore when they hurt each other. But they don't stay there. They're willing to listen and forgive.

We also have to offer grace and be hard to offend. All of us get prickly when we're exhausted, hungry, or not feeling well. We get hit with friendly fire that doesn't have anything to do with us.

Don't be grouchy. Learn to laugh at yourself and with each other.

THREE: COMMUNICATE YOUR LOVE FOR EACH OTHER.

Your spouse, your parents, your siblings, or your children don't know you love them until you show it. It's one thing to feel it, but for them to experience it, it has to come out of you in a way they can receive.

You could say all four of the commands listed in this passage challenge us to speak life to each other instead of being disrespectful or discouraging.

In most families, the other members receive love differently than we do. You may prefer physical touch (a hug, holding hands, etc.) while they may prefer quality time, words of affirmation, acts of service, or gifts. For love to be received in the most meaningful way, offer it in the way they receive it instead of the way you like to give it.

So, write a note. Send a text. Plan a special afternoon together. Do something around the house unexpectedly. Reach over and grab their hand. Surprise them with that special something they didn't think you remembered.

Families that live together this way experience the peace of God in their homes.

Discussion

Read Colossians 3:18-21: [18] Wives, submit yourselves to your husbands, as is fitting in the Lord. [19] Husbands, love your wives and do not be harsh with them. [20] Children, obey your parents in everything, for this pleases the Lord. [21] Fathers, do not embitter your children, or they will become discouraged.

1. How is "family" both a blessing and a challenge sometimes?

2. Read verse 18. Why does God begin by addressing wives? What does it mean for wives to submit to their husbands?

3. Read verse 19. How can husbands love their wives? Why is this important?

4. Verse 19 instructs husbands not to be harsh with their wives. Of all the things Paul could have said here, why do you think he told husbands not to be harsh?

5. If you are married, how would you grade yourself against verses 18-19? Explain.

6. Read verse 20. According to this verse, what is the reason children should obey their parents? Why is this important?

7. Read verse 21. What do you think it means to embitter your children? How can you guard against doing that?

8. Why is forgiveness important for family unity?

9. Think of a time you needed to forgive someone in your family or when you needed forgiveness. What happened?

Questions

Application

People don't know you love them until you show it.

Use the space below to write the names of each person in your immediate family.

Then ask: How can I show each person listed that I love them this week?

Next to each name, write down what you will do. Pray and ask God to help you love the people closest to you this week.

Prayer

God, I know You have a plan for our family. Help us to follow Your plan as we love and give thanks to You. I'm asking You to bless my spouse, to fill them with Your presence and Your love, and help my kids to discover and walk in the life You've created them to live. In Jesus' name, Amen.

We encourage you to make this prayer your own. Include the family members or circumstances that fit for you. This isn't about what family you have or don't have, it's how you love and serve the people God's placed you with.

Week Six

06.

YOUR *WORK*

THEME VERSE

Whatever you do, work at it with all your heart, as working for the Lord, not for human masters.

Colossians 3:23

KEY TRUTH

Life on Purpose makes all work spiritual—no matter our specific job.

PASSAGE

Colossians 3:23-24

CONCEPT

IT ***doesn't matter*** HOW OLD YOU ARE, WHERE ***you're from,*** WHERE ***you went to school,*** OR WHAT ***your parents did or didn't do***—EVERY ONE OF US ***wants to be successful.***

- **We want to feel like we made a difference.**
- **We want to be an integral part of something special.**
- **We want our lives to count.**

And many of us look to our career or our work as the primary means to reach these goals.

!

Life on Purpose makes all work spiritual.

The problem is, our work almost always leaves us lacking.

We often find ourselves frustrated with our boss . . . or our employees.

The overwhelming majority of workers feel like their contributions are unrecognized. It's the number one reason people quit their jobs. Global work disengagement—the feeling of not caring about what you do—hovers around 80%.

This is tragic.

We give our energy and our time to an atmosphere, and we're not sure what we have to show for it.

So, we spend a large percentage of our lives feeling frustrated and dissatisfied.

We have a complicated relationship with work. Some people view it as a necessary evil as they daydream about quitting their jobs and retiring to a life of doing nothing.

Others treat their work and career as an idol—they look to it for meaning, fulfillment, identity, and validation.

Both of these extremes are incapable of leading us to the life we were created to live.

For some, it's because they're expecting too much from their career.

For others, they haven't applied themselves and allowed God to develop the gifts and talents He has entrusted to them.

***Life on Purpose* makes all work spiritual.**

When we're in Christ, He comes with us to our workplace, no matter our occupation.

Therefore, our character, our competency, and the way we approach what we do every day in our career is a reflection of our relationship with God.

Colossians 3:23 tells us that whatever we do, no matter what our job is, we should do it with all our hearts, with our best effort, with our best attitude, because we're doing it for God, not for a paycheck or our boss.

Whatever you do, work at it with all your heart, as working for the Lord, not for human masters.

Colossians 3:23

✦ ✦ ✦

Work can be found in the very first chapter of the Bible. Before there were humans, God was working. And He delighted in His work.

And although He never tires or changes and is eternally self-sufficient, God chose to rest.

[2] By the seventh day God had finished the work he had been doing; so on the seventh day he rested from all his work. [3] Then God blessed the seventh day and made it holy, because on it he rested from all the work of creating that he had done.

Genesis 2:2-3

It's almost as if the resting allowed Him to more fully delight in the work He did the next day. One of the first things He did was instruct us to follow His pattern.

Because He is a good and loving God, He invites us into the family business of taking care of God's good creation—the foundation for all work. The Bible calls this concept "stewardship."

Here's a simple summary of stewardship:

Everything we have is a gift from God. Therefore, what we do with it is our gift to Him.

This is why the Hebrew word for "work" shares the same root as the word for "worship." That's what our work was designed to be: worship.

"Cursed is the ground because of you; through painful toil you will eat food from it all the days of your life."

Genesis 3:17b

But like it does with everything else, sin destroys the beauty and health of work. We see the consequences of this in Genesis 3. One of the consequences of sin given to Adam was that his work became infinitely more difficult, tedious, and painful.

Do you see someone skilled in their work? They will serve before kings; they will not serve before officials of low rank.

Proverbs 22:29

The Bible has a lot to say about work—Proverbs tells us there's profit in all hard work and that those who are skilled in their work will stand before kings. In 1 Thessalonians 5:12, Paul says to "acknowledge those who work hard among you," and to hold them in the highest honor.

"His master replied, 'Well done, good and faithful servant! You have been faithful with a few things; I will put you in charge of many things. Come and share your master's happiness!'"

Matthew 25:23

Jesus talked many times about being a good and faithful steward. This concept was at the center of many of His parables.

Matthew 25 is a definitive teaching on the subject. It captures the essence of how Jesus talked about stewardship.

He tells the story of a master who gives five bags of gold to one person, two to another, and one to a third. When the master returns, he wants to know what the workers have done with what they've been given.

The man with five bags of gold put them to work and made five more. The man with two bags also put them to work and doubled the investment. But the man with one bag of gold felt sorry for himself, and in his fear of his boss, he hid the bag of gold.

The master takes the bag of gold from this man and gives it to the first man with ten before he throws out the disgruntled worker.

The ending of this story rolls right into another story where Jesus talks about the end of time and the great judgment when each of us will stand before Him and give an account of what we've done with what we've been given.

Our perspective on work determines our level of fulfillment.

If we choose to work for ourselves and only our career ambitions, it is likely we'll live constantly longing for the next thing.

If we choose to work for our boss or employer as our source, it is likely we'll constantly compare ourselves to others and feel like we're being mistreated.

EVERYTHING WE HAVE IS A GIFT FROM GOD. THEREFORE, WHAT WE DO WITH IT IS OUR GIFT TO HIM.

If we choose to work for God, we can trust Him to generously meet all of our needs, to promote us, and to find the unique fulfillment only afforded to those who offer their gifts to advance His Kingdom.

When we make this choice, we discover all work is spiritual. God doesn't ask us to get a new job; we can honor Him with our work, right where we are.

CONTEXT

If the language of servants, masters, and even slaves has been bothering you, this is understandable. Throughout history, people have misinterpreted and misapplied what the Bible is saying on this issue.

Remember, just as we did with women and children in Week 5, in order to properly understand what's happening, we have to go back to the cultural context of when this letter was written.

Servants and slaves were an accepted part of the ancient world. Unlike the transatlantic slave trade, it was not primarily based on race, and servants could earn their freedom over time.

None of this condones the notion of one human being "owning" another, a concept that completely opposes the biblical view of human beings having inherent worth and value because every human being is created in the image of God. When Paul directly addresses this group on multiple occasions in the letter, it emphasizes their dignity and honors their contribution.

It validates God's desire to include them in ***Life on Purpose***—the life they were created to live.

Perhaps it feels like a stretch to compare these relationships to our modern workplace environment, but this all depends on who you ask and how they feel their company treats them. It's not a perfect equivalent, but the wisdom and insight from the Holy Spirit's words to them are still meaningful and life-giving to each of us.

✦ ✦ ✦

This famous passage in Colossians has a fascinating backstory. Most Bible scholars believe the subtext of this passage is what's often considered a companion letter to Colossians—the book of Philemon.

The book of Philemon is an incredibly rich, relationally-complicated one-chapter book in the New Testament. Philemon was a close friend of Paul's who loved God and helped the cause of the early church, including this group of believers in Colossae.

Philemon had a falling out with one of his servants named

Onesimus. The Bible doesn't tell us what happened, but this servant runs away and ends up in prison with Paul. There, he gives his life to Christ, becomes a great help to Paul, and they become spiritual family.

As a result, Paul now loves both Philemon and Onesimus—a former servant and his master who have a serious relational issue. Paul's response is to send a letter to his friend Philemon, delivered by the very servant who ended up in prison as a result of their relational challenges.

The moment Onesimus comes back to Philemon with the letter from Paul had to have been incredibly emotional and highly awkward.

But Paul believed it was what God wanted because it serves as a great picture of healthy relationships in the workplace.

The letter does not go to great lengths to determine precisely what happened and who was ultimately at fault or offer a detailed plan for justice.

Instead, there is a general appeal to the greater reality that both men made mistakes. God had been gracious, generous, and forgiving to both, and as a result, both should extend this same kindness and forgiveness to each other.

Whether you are the servant or the master, whether you are the employer or the employee, the boss or the entry-level worker, if you're in Christ, this should be the defining characteristic of your work life.

In Christ, you work for the Lord with all your heart, independent of how others treat you or the quality of the assignment, because you trust your reward will come from Him.

Paul reminds Philemon he could command him to forgive Onesimus, but he appeals to his maturity instead. He asks him to receive this servant as a brother in Christ, and if there is any challenge or issue, he should charge it to Paul.

Finally, Paul writes that he hopes to come see both of them in the near future in order to celebrate the restoration of their relationship.

[17] So if you consider me a partner, welcome him as you would welcome me. [18] If he has done you any wrong or owes you anything, charge it to me.

Philemon 1:17-18

Colossians 3:23-24

23 Whatever you do, work at it with all your
heart, as working for the Lord, not for human
masters, 24 since you know that you will receive
an inheritance from the Lord as a reward. It is
the Lord Christ you are serving.

WHAT DOES THIS MEAN FOR US?

Because God created us, He knows what we need.

When we faithfully steward the gifts, opportunities, and responsibilities He has entrusted to us, we experience fulfillment, other people are blessed by our contribution, and God is glorified through the process.

That's what we're all searching for.

Unfortunately, most people don't experience this. Instead, they're left to struggle with the all-too-common realities of the workplace.

One person said there are three kinds of people in every business: people who make everything about them (takers), people who do things for coworkers when coworkers do things for them (matchers), and people who try to help their coworkers regardless of what they do for them (givers).

We've all had experiences with each of these types of co-workers.

People who put themselves first are the most dissatisfied, people who do for others when others do for them are the most common, but people who are willing to help others within reason are the most fulfilled.

If we only try to help others to win their favor or to feel good about ourselves, we'll likely take on more than we can handle and it will end up keeping us from doing our own work.

But when we see ourselves properly, when we're working for the Lord, we're able to steward our responsibility first while being willing to help our teammates however we can. Not only is this personally rewarding, but in healthy environments it creates great value for the team.

What Do I Do with This?

Tomorrow (or the next day you go to work), remember your primary responsibility is not to your direct report, the owner of the company (even if it's you!), or the shareholders.

Your first responsibility is to the God who created you, who entrusted you with talents and abilities, who gave you life and put the breath in your lungs.

Promotion comes from the Lord. Think of Joseph or Daniel and his friends. They were mistreated and sabotaged by terrible bosses, but God continued to promote them and give them favor.

ONE: WORK FOR THE LORD.

No matter your industry or career, you can offer your best effort and develop your skills out of your love for God.

TWO: DON'T LET YOUR WORK DEFINE YOU.

You're more than what you do, your accomplishments and titles, or your income level. The work itself has value and meaning, but work can't give YOU value and meaning.

THREE: ADD VALUE TO OTHERS.

Be the best teammate you can be, not so others will love and affirm you, but because God already does.

Discussion

Read Colossians 3:23-24: 23 Whatever you do, work at it with all your heart, as working for the Lord, not for human masters, 24 since you know that you will receive an inheritance from the Lord as a reward. It is the Lord Christ you are serving.

1. How do you feel about your current job? Be honest. Are you satisfied and fulfilled? Explain. If you do not currently work for a paycheck (ie. student, stay-at-home parent, retiree), how do you feel about your current life stage?

2. What does God desire work to be like for us?

3. Read Colossians 3:23-24 again. According to these verses, who do you ultimately work for? How does understanding this change how you view your job?

4. Do you currently see your job as a stewardship before God? How faithful are you being with that stewardship?

5. Do you ever struggle with letting work define you? Explain.

6. How can we find fulfillment in work without letting it define us?

7. At every job there are takers, matchers, and givers. Which of those terms best describes you? How can you grow in this area?

Questions

Application

Take a moment to think of three people you work with or interact with on a regular basis, and ask yourself:

How can I add value to each of these people this week?

Write down their names and what you will do. ***Pray and commit your plan to God.***

Prayer

Lord, I understand all work is spiritual when we do it for You. Help me to honor You with the way I work each day, through my excellence, in my attitude, and the way I serve others. I want to walk in everything You have for me in this area of my life and to experience the fulfillment and purpose You have for me. In Your name I pray, Amen.

Week Seven

07.

MAKE THE *MOST* OF *EVERY* OPPORTUNITY

THEME VERSE

Be wise in the way you act toward outsiders; make the most of every opportunity.

Colossians 4:5

KEY TRUTH

Life on Purpose inspires us to be gracious and considerate in the way we treat people.

PASSAGE

Colossians 4:5-6

CONCEPT

WE LIVE IN A ***polarized age. The internet and social media*** ALLOW US TO ***quickly and easily find people who agree*** WITH OUR POLITICAL AND ***personal preferences.***

It also makes it easier than ever before to shut down and keep out people who think and believe differently than us.

It's not healthy—especially for followers of Christ.

There have always been, and will always be, people around us who are not like us. As followers of Christ, we don't have the

Life on Purpose inspires us to be gracious and considerate in the way we treat people.

right or the privilege to ignore or vilify them.

Jesus didn't leave us that option.

From the very beginning, followers of Christ have loved, served, respected, and made room for people from different religious, political, and cultural backgrounds.

This does not mean they affirm and endorse these beliefs. In fact, it's the opposite.

Genuine Christians are not threatened, surprised, or intimidated when others do not share their beliefs. They strengthen their own convictions as they commit to love and pray for those who disagree.

***Life on Purpose* inspires us to be gracious and considerate in the way we treat people.**

Colossians 4:5 instructs us to be wise in the way we act toward outsiders so we can make the most of every opportunity.

We can't expect people who don't know and love God to act like people who do.

Especially people who boldly declare or celebrate their differences. It's not wise to act or treat them in a way that jeopardizes the one opportunity we may have to impact them with the love and message of Jesus.

Be wise in the way you act toward outsiders; make the most of every opportunity.

Colossians 4:5

This does not condone or approve of their actions and attitudes, but it acknowledges a different set of expectations, which gives us room to be gracious.

This has been one of the defining character traits of the body of Christ. This phrase, "the body of Christ," is more than another name for the Church or the people of God.

It means that after Jesus ascended into heaven and gave His followers the Great Commission to make disciples wherever they go, we are now Jesus' hands and feet on the earth.

> [19] "Therefore go and make disciples of all nations, baptizing them in the name of the Father and of the Son and of the Holy Spirit, [20] and teaching them to obey everything I have commanded you. And surely I am with you always, to the very end of the age."
>
> **Matthew 28:19-20**

If they're going to see Him, it's going to be through us. This doesn't mean we're perfect or that we don't make mistakes, but it creates a picture of how we aspire to live.

On His last night with His disciples, Jesus prayed for them in a garden in the moments leading up to His betrayal and arrest. These were important prayers, and because He's so generous, chapter 17 of the Gospel of John tells us what He prayed.

Jesus prayed and asked God to help His disciples love each other the way He had loved them because He believed if the world saw them live this way, they would recognize them as followers of Jesus.

> [20] "My prayer is not for them alone. I pray also for those who will believe in me through their message, [21] that all of them may be one, Father, just as you are in me and I am in you . . . [23] I in them and you in me—so that they may be brought to complete unity. Then the world will know that you sent me and have loved them even as you have loved me. Then the world will know that you sent me and have loved them even as you have loved me."
>
> **John 17:20-21a, 23**

✦ ✦ ✦

Today, perhaps more than ever, gracious, kind, and considerate people stand out. They surprise us. They leave a lasting impression.

This should be an easy target for followers of Christ to hit. We don't need all the answers to every theological question. We don't have to always know what to say.

But we can be gracious and kind. That goal is not beyond our reach.

Perhaps it seems basic or obvious, but a church is meant to be much more than a holy huddle gathered together trying to keep the world out.

A church is a gathered collection of God's people who demonstrate the love of God and His kindness in a way others can receive it. Especially those who are new, who are coming from a different perspective, and who are nervous and uncertain about this God and His people.

According to Jesus, they should expect love and kindness. Unfortunately, those are often the last things they expect.

The largest research project ever conducted into why people stop going to church discovered the primary reason wasn't political or even theological—it was relational.

You may be surprised that the single greatest reason people stopped going to church was that they moved to a different area. As our society continues to be more mobile, life gets disrupted by a new address, a new routine, and new daily responsibilities.

For many people, it's not that they stopped being open to God.

They're simply trying to help their family adjust to a new location, new circumstances, and a new way of doing life.

In fact, most of them would come back if they had a friend to help them navigate the transition.

Most people don't expect everyone else to think like them. What they're hoping for is to know someone sees them, someone understands, and someone cares.

Life is challenging and complicated. We all need encouragement. When we find someone who gives us hope and helps us see our circumstances differently, we're grateful.

We all need those kinds of people in our lives.

And we can all be those kinds of people—even with those we think we have nothing in common with.

CONTEXT

In Colossians 4, Paul is summarizing his letter and beginning his closing remarks to the church in Colossae. He instructs them to remain devoted to prayer first and foremost, for their own benefit and spiritual development.

And then he asks them to pray for him. Remember, Paul is not sitting in a comfortable office presiding over the affairs of the New Testament church.

Once again he has found himself in prison because of the impact of his ministry—a situation he was all too familiar with. But he was also keenly aware of God's miraculous power to throw open prison doors and save both prisoners and jailers alike.

In Week 6, we learned how this particular prison sentence afforded him the opportunity to facilitate significant relational reconciliation between a member of the church named Philemon and his runaway servant Onesimus.

The amazing thing is, we're reading this letter today because Onesimus delivered it to the people in Colossae.[5]

What Paul's asking them to pray for is an open door for the message of Jesus, and the ability to proclaim this message clearly. While this is Paul's unique assignment in the communication of the gospel, the task is not his alone.

His next few remarks give tremendous insight into the general disposition he wanted from the people in the church as part of their role in communicating the gospel.

Paul gives us excellent coaching on how we should relate to people who think differently from us. These wise words are incredibly helpful for us today.

[3] And pray for us, too, that God may open a door for our message, so that we may proclaim the mystery of Christ, for which I am in chains. [4] Pray that I may proclaim it clearly, as I should.

Colossians 4:3-4

[5] Along with Paul's ministry associate Tychicus.

Colossians 4:5-6

5 Be wise in the way you act toward outsiders;
make the most of every opportunity. 6 Let your
conversation be always full of grace, seasoned
with salt, so that you may know how to answer
everyone.

WHAT DOES THIS MEAN FOR US?

The passage begins with the challenge to be wise in the way you act toward outsiders. Unfortunately, followers of Christ have often been accused of being self-righteous, hypocritical, judgmental, angry, and mean.

None of these would be considered wise. Wisdom toward outsiders requires us to be self-aware, especially of our flaws, quirks, idiosyncrasies, and contradictions. This is where the relational masterclass from Week 3 can serve us well.

We should be able to not take ourselves too seriously and be the first to laugh at ourselves. We should consider how we might interpret our actions, attitudes, and responses if we were the other person.

These may sound basic, but too often, they can be overlooked by well-intended people so focused on being "right" about the issues that they forget how to be right with the person.

Basic wisdom requires the consideration to stop and think, *Am I acting in a way that represents the heart of Jesus? Am I giving this person a reason to get offended or upset?*

Next, the Holy Spirit reminds us through Paul to make the most of every opportunity. In his letter to the Ephesians, we can find the exact same challenge. None of us are promised tomorrow.

What may seem like an ordinary, typical conversation could be the last meaningful interaction with a person.

This is not meant to scare us or make us nervous, but to give us an appreciation for the potential eternal significance available to us in every moment.

Essentially, even our conversations are an expression of the stewardship we described in Week 6. God loves outsiders—we see this pattern over and over throughout Scripture. Nothing causes a greater celebration in heaven than when an outsider comes home.

[15] Be very careful, then, how you live—not as unwise but as wise, [16] making the most of every opportunity, because the days are evil.

Ephesians 5:15-16

Therefore, when He entrusts us to represent Him in an interaction with someone He deeply cares for, He wants us to steward those conversations well because we will give an account for what we said or didn't say.

"But I tell you that everyone will have to give account on the day of judgment for every empty word they have spoken."

Matthew 12:36

Notice Paul describes our actions with outsiders as conversations. He didn't say to shout at them until they repent. Conversations move back and forth. They require an exchange. It means we should listen instead of merely waiting for our turn to talk again.

And these conversations should always be filled with grace. This means we are to be emotionally generous (quick to listen, slow to get angry, hard to offend, willing to carefully consider a perspective we disagree with, etc.).

Bible scholars suggest that the phrase "seasoned with salt" is an old Jewish idiom that means to keep things interesting, never boring or bland. Enjoyable conversations spark laughter, joy, intrigue, and surprise. They're not boring monologues.

A helpful tip for having meaningful conversations is to be more concerned with being interested than interesting. Everyone enjoys talking with an active listener, who pays attention, responds, and asks thoughtful follow-up questions.

People who always turn the conversation back to themselves or who try to top every story or anecdote with one of their own aren't enjoyable to talk to.

Finally, the passage ends with the most daunting challenge—knowing how to answer everyone. Is that all?!

On our own, none of us know how to answer everyone.

But when we treat every conversation as a gift from God, each interaction as a divine opportunity to represent His love to someone potentially far from Him with grace and wisdom, we'll be amazed at what He does through us.

19 My dear brothers and sisters, take note of this: Everyone should be quick to listen, slow to speak and slow to become angry, 20 because human anger does not produce the righteousness that God desires.

James 1:19-20

What Do I Do with This?

Most of us want time to be prepared for important conversations. But the point of this passage is to convey that they can happen at any time and any place.

That's why we need to be wise. We never know when our next interaction with an outsider will take place, so we've got to always be ready.

How can we be ready?

ONE: BE AWARE— ESPECIALLY SELF-AWARE.

If we're not careful, we can treat people around us as strangers who exist as a means to our end. Followers of Christ don't see people as strangers, but potential friends we haven't met yet. In order to treat people this way, we have to remember the world doesn't revolve around us. We start with consideration.

TWO: FOCUS ON BEING INTERESTED INSTEAD OF INTERESTING.

Trying to sound significant or important isn't gracious or wise. We all know what it feels like to be around this person. Remember, a conversation is a back-and-forth interaction. Be an active listener. Add more value than you take.

THREE: SEE CONVERSATIONS AS ETERNALLY SIGNIFICANT.

We are stewards who have been entrusted with the responsibility of representing God to people. One day we'll give an account to God. This reality should not make us fearful or anxious but give us hope to do our part. A kind word, a listening ear, or an encouraging thought can be our contribution in God's desire to communicate His love to the person in front of us. That's how we make the most of every opportunity.

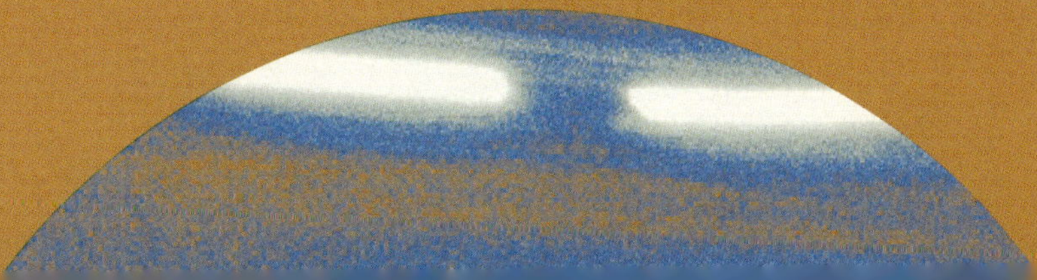

Discussion

Read Colossians 4:5-6: [5] Be wise in the way you act toward outsiders; make the most of every opportunity. [6] Let your conversation be always full of grace, seasoned with salt, so that you may know how to answer everyone.

1. Verse 5 tells us to be wise in how we act toward outsiders. What does that mean?

2. What's the opposite of being wise in our interactions with others?

3. Verse 5 also tells us to make the most of every opportunity. Why is this important, especially when talking with those who are not believers?

4. In your social interactions, do you treat people more as a means to an end, or do you value people and consider what is best for them? Explain.

5. What does it mean to have your conversations "seasoned with salt"? What are some practical things you can do to grow in this area?

6. When having conversations, do you think more about what you're going to say or about what the other person is saying? Explain.

7. What are ways we can add value to others when talking or interacting with them?

Questions

Application

Think of someone you know who does not know Christ.

What can you do this week to engage with and add value to this person?

Prayer

Jesus, I believe ***Life on Purpose*** inspires us to be gracious and considerate toward outsiders. Help me to be wise so that every interaction with someone who thinks differently is an opportunity for them to want to know You more. In Your name, Amen.

SCRIPTURE MEMORY CARDS & KEY TRUTHS

These Scripture memory cards and key truths correspond to each week in the *Life on Purpose* study.

We encourage you to memorize the theme verse each week of *Life on Purpose*. To help, detach these cards and put them somewhere visible, like the dash of your car, the back of your phone, your desk at work, or your bathroom mirror.

We also encourage you to detach the key truth card and use it as a bookmark for this guide or place it somewhere visible.

LIFE ON PURPOSE

COLOSSIANS 1:27

To them God
has chosen to make
known among the
Gentiles the glorious
riches of this
mystery, which is
Christ in you,
the hope of glory.

INTRODUCTION

COLOSSIANS 1:28

He is the one
we proclaim,
admonishing and
teaching everyone
with all wisdom,
so that we may
present everyone
fully mature in Christ.

WEEK ONE:
CHRIST *IN YOU*

COLOSSIANS 3:3

For you died,
and your life is now
hidden with
Christ in God.

WEEK TWO:
YOUR *THINKING*

COLOSSIANS 3:12

Therefore, as God's
chosen people,
holy and dearly
loved, clothe
yourselves with
compassion,
kindness, humility,
gentleness and
patience.

WEEK THREE:
YOUR *RELATIONSHIPS*

COLOSSIANS 3:15

Let the peace of
Christ rule in
your hearts, since
as members of
one body you were
called to peace.
And be thankful.

WEEK FOUR:
YOUR *PEACE*

COLOSSIANS 3:17

And whatever
you do, whether in
word or deed, do
it all in the name of
the Lord Jesus, giving
thanks to God the
Father through him.

WEEK FIVE:
YOUR *FAMILY*

COLOSSIANS 3:23

Whatever you do,
work at it with
all your heart,
as working for the
Lord, not for
human masters.

WEEK SIX:
YOUR *WORK*

COLOSSIANS 4:5

Be wise in the
way you act toward
outsiders; make
the most of every
opportunity.

WEEK SEVEN:
MAKE THE *MOST* OF
EVERY OPPORTUNITY

LIFE ON PURPOSE

LIFE ON PURPOSE

LIFE ON PURPOSE

LIFE ON PURPOSE

LIFE ON PURPOSE

LIFE ON PURPOSE

LIFE ON PURPOSE

LIFE ON PURPOSE

KEYS TO A
LIFE ON PURPOSE

INTRODUCTION

Life on Purpose is intentional, meaningful, and comes from the One who created us.

WEEK 1 | CHRIST *IN YOU*

Life on Purpose is only found in Christ.

WEEK 2 | YOUR *THINKING*

Life on Purpose requires us to align our thoughts with God's Word.

WEEK 3 | YOUR *RELATIONSHIPS*

Life on Purpose promotes healthy relationships.

WEEK 4 | YOUR *PEACE*

Life on Purpose prioritizes peace over our emotions and desires.

WEEK 5 | YOUR *FAMILY*

Life on Purpose follows God's plan for our families.

WEEK 6 | YOUR *WORK*

Life on Purpose makes all work spiritual—no matter our specific job.

WEEK 7 | MAKE THE *MOST* OF *EVERY* OPPORTUNITY

Life on Purpose inspires us to be gracious and considerate in the way we treat people.

LIFE ON PURPOSE